UNCOMMON COURAGE

UNCOMMON COURAGE

KEISHA TONI RUSSELL

HARVEST HOUSE PUBLISHERS
EUGENE. OREGON

Cover design by Faceout Studio

Cover image © Faceout Studio, Elisha Zepeda

Back cover author photo by John Kringas Photography

Interior design by KUHN Design Group

For bulk, special sales, or ministry purchases, please call 1-800-547-8979.
Email: CustomerService@hhpbooks.com

This logo is a federally registered trademark of the Hawkins Children's LLC. Harvest House Publishers, Inc., is the exclusive licensee of this trademark.

Uncommon Courage
Copyright © 2024 by Keisha Toni Russell
Published by Harvest House Publishers
Eugene, Oregon 97408
www.harvesthousepublishers.com

ISBN 978-0-7369-8640-3 (pbk)
ISBN 978-0-7369-8641-0 (eBook)

Library of Congress Control Number: 2023938673

Printed in the United States of America

24 25 26 27 28 29 30 31 32 / BP / 10 9 8 7 6 5 4 3 2 1

To my mom and sister. I miss you both.

"Always be ready to make your defense to anyone who demands from you an accounting for the hope that is in you, yet do it with gentleness and respect."

1 PETER 3:15-16

FREEDOM IS A CENTRAL
PRINCIPLE OF CHRISTIANITY,
AND THAT PRINCIPLE THRIVES
IN A CULTURE THAT EMBRACES
THE FREEDOM OF RELIGION.

KEISHA TONI RUSSELL

CONTENTS

TESTIFY

When a jury assesses a case, they must analyze the evidence and decide which side wins. A witness's testimony brings clarity to a case because they can provide a firsthand account. But testifying is not always easy. It's something most people must be forced to do.

When the disciples told people about what they experienced with Jesus, it cost many of them their lives. But they were compelled to testify. As Christians, we are commanded to tell our testimony to the world. We are expected to proclaim who Christ is and how He has changed our lives. And it's not just about what we say. The way we live our lives reveals to others the strength and depth of our relationship with Christ, or lack thereof. Our behavior tells a story to nonbelievers about Christians. But it also has the power to edify, inform, and inspire other believers to persevere with Christ.

I share my testimony to persuade the nonbeliever and strengthen the believer.

Like most people who end up in a spiritual fight, I didn't pursue it. I was called.

My journey began right after I graduated from undergraduate school and became an educator in Atlanta. I worked in a vocational college where I realized that many of the students were grossly unprepared for college. Many of them couldn't read or write at a high school level, and most of them were deficient in their math skills. Having obtained a strong public education myself, I wondered why our nation's system had failed these students. After a few years of working with college students, God sent me to teach elementary students, where He opened my eyes to some of the issues plaguing our public school system.

After getting a master's degree in teaching from the University of Southern California, I joined Teach For America, an organization that seeks high-achieving college graduates to commit to expanding educational opportunities for low-income students by teaching for at least two years in a public school. Their goal is to close the academic achievement gap that persists between wealthy and mostly white students and poor minorities. I was assigned to teach elementary special education in Atlanta Public Schools.

I started the school year by assessing my fourth- and fifth-grade special education students in reading and math. Their scores were devastating. All the students were several grade levels behind. This isn't uncommon for special education students, but I was disheartened at the reality of their scores. I knew the students' futures would be severely limited if they couldn't even read.

I also found out that the students possessed ingrained beliefs about education and themselves that negatively affected their self-esteem. Many of them grew up watching friends and relatives who did not take school seriously, and the students did not understand why they should give their education more of their attention. I was keenly aware that these students were in a predominately black part of Atlanta, with nearly all black teachers and administrators, and those leaders had allowed these students to continue through school without getting the basics skills. Not to mention that some of the students' lives at home were challenging for various reasons.

The students' challenges couldn't be blamed directly on systemic racism or white supremacy because they rarely encountered anyone white. However, it was clear there was a generational mindset producing at least some of the bad fruit I was seeing.

I was successful at teaching the students how to read, and many of them passed the state tests for the first time in their lives, even though they were in fourth or fifth grade at the time. Later in the book I talk about how I accomplished this, but this classroom taught me how to be an advocate and an educator. While I was teaching, I knew that there was lots of work to do in the education system, but I felt led to learn how to be a more powerful advocate.

After teaching for a few years and being nominated for a teacher-of-the-year award, I applied to law school. I didn't initially plan to attend Emory Law, but as I browsed the websites for different law schools in Georgia, Emory stood out. I was drawn to their Center for the Study of Law and Religion. No other school had anything comparable, and I was fascinated by the intersection of the two disciplines.

Like most law schools, Emory was a largely liberal environment. The students, professors, and most of the administrators were mostly left-leaning and their lectures often reflected their political views. This was not a big deal to me except when I thought a professor's views influenced the classroom discussions, specifically in connection with issues like criminal justice, abortion, and same-sex unions.

My first semester, I enrolled in a clinic where I learned advocacy on behalf of foster children at the Georgia legislature during the 2015 legislative session. We drafted bills and worked on influencing senators and representatives to pass bills that would help children. The best part of this experience was being there on the last night of the session when the bell rang. We left the capital in the middle of the night, and I experienced a euphoria from the energy of the environment that I didn't think I'd ever experience with politics.

After my stint with the children's advocacy clinic, I quickly transitioned to being more involved in the Center. Up until that point, I edited research papers and treatises and wrote papers for my Religion and Law class. By 2016, I was a research assistant for Dr. Mark Goldfeder, an adjunct professor at Emory, the head of the student programs in the Center, and international counsel for the American Center for Law and Justice.

Around the same time, I was writing a paper charging Christians to be more involved in the education system. I was studying some of the work of critical race theorists and how those views could inform the problem. I found that critical theory did not present workable solutions. It also conflicted constantly with what I experienced as a teacher. This was a reminder that theory does not always align with practice. I finished the paper, but I was unsettled with my findings.

Meanwhile, it was an election year, and the media was extremely polarized between Hillary Clinton and Donald Trump. A constant theme in the news was police shootings involving black men. The reports were plastered on the television nearly every week leading up to the election. This exacerbated the mood of already-stressed-out students at the law school, and especially affected the black male law students. They were noticeably more tense, despondent, and frustrated. I couldn't help but wonder why the coverage was suddenly more intense. The reports felt politically manipulative, but at that point, I was not clear about why.

For the most part, I stayed away from the news and read news articles only when they covered popular subjects or when I was working on a project and I wanted to see the news coverage. I often noticed that there was a clear rift between what the news coverage said and the facts of the issue. This would be the beginning of my awakening to the deception that commonly takes place in the news.

As election day drew closer, the media coverage was intense, but most people seemed confident that Hillary Clinton would win. All the polls pointed in her favor. After Donald Trump astonishingly won the election, one of my professors cried in class about the results. One of the student groups laid out crayons and coloring books in the hallways and student center area of the law school building that allowed students to vent if they were feeling especially stressed about the election results.

I can't say that I was excited about Donald Trump's win. I thought he was brash and uncouth, but I wasn't a fan of Hillary Clinton either. To me, choosing between the two was difficult. So I was ambivalent to the election results. I knew that no matter who won the election, my mission was still the same. I had no idea then how much Donald Trump's win would impact the next few years of my life.

Immediately after the election, American Center for Law & Justice's work shifted because its president, Jay Sekulow, became a new member of Trump's legal team. I researched and drafted memos and briefs for many of the first set of legal issues facing the administration. There were a myriad of lawsuits and challenges. I also worked on a few confirmation hearings for the presidential appointments. It was complex, high-impact work.

At the same time, we also conducted research for Israel while the country led the legal committee of the United Nations. I can't say much about the substance of the work, but it was beyond interesting, and I learned a great deal about foreign policy. The work never stopped, and I was grateful to be learning so much as a third-year law student. I knew very few of my classmates were learning the law at the level I was.

Most of my classmates were unaware of the scope of my work. I didn't talk about it much, mostly because I couldn't. But many of them were discouraging about whether I should pursue constitutional law as a career. One of them told me I needed to try to get "a real job." I wondered what she was doing in her summer internships, because I knew it didn't compare to the work I was doing at that point.

I was able to get a job as a constitutional lawyer immediately out of law school. It was a divinely orchestrated situation. Mark Goldfeder at Emory connected me with First Liberty Institute, a religious liberty law firm. This led to an internship, and eventually, I was hired as a full-time lawyer. I was one of the first attorneys at the organization hired directly out of law school.

As a religious liberty lawyer, I became intimately involved in the conflicts between the culture and the church. I could see how the increasing liberalization of society was causing people to express disdain for Christian principles and any proclamations of moral absolutes. The cultural trend was infecting state and federal governments, corporations, the news, education, and more. Christians who hold to a firmly biblical perspective are not only in the minority; they are the despised minority. The lawsuits we handled and the accompanying deceptive media coverage about those lawsuits revealed to me that the country is in flux. While the Bible warns us that the world will hate Christians, it is still alarming to watch America's rabid disdain for religion, and for Christianity in particular.

When you work on the front lines of the culture wars, you learn to discern the truth from the lies in the media. Over the last several years of working as a constitutional lawyer, I learned a lot about how the media manipulates the public. I would read the coverage about our cases and realize that the media was doing its best to portray the religious as the enemies in the conflict. The mainstream media rarely covered our cases in a positive light. The manipulation was effective because I realized that even Christians believed what the media told them.

Judges also become extremely important when you are a lawyer, especially a constitutional lawyer. The types of cases we worked on could often impact the law for some or all of the country. I learned that the judicial philosophy of a judge is imperative. First Liberty started evaluating Donald Trump's picks for the federal judiciary from the beginning of his presidency. Sometimes we approved his picks; sometimes we didn't. We weren't always on the good side of either political party because of our decision to evaluate each judge neutrally. But we knew that our evaluation needed to be sound. We did what we knew most people were not doing.

We read everything those prospective picks had ever written. We looked at their speeches and the organizations they belonged to. We evaluated every aspect of their professional lives and rated the judges as objectively as possible.

This is why when the Biden administration picked Ketanji Brown Jackson as a nominee for the US Supreme Court, it was just business as usual for us. We did what we had been doing for years. We looked at her and the other prospective choices and, unsurprisingly, concluded that they were all fairly liberal advocacy judges whose beliefs would likely lead them to erroneously interpret the law and the Constitution in order to advance political objectives. Justice Jackson was problematic on many levels.

I spoke to many Christians about Jackson and realized that they knew nothing about her, yet had completely accepted the media's narratives about why they should support her. They didn't think that those in the news media would deceive them. Later, I'll provide more details to support my conclusions about her. But this experience related to Justice Jackson was one of many that I encountered that made me realize the church trusts the world far too much.

During the past decade, the culture's respect for morality and especially religion has depleted to a dangerously low level. Those who have biblical views are compared to the worst people in history, like Hitler and white supremacists. The nation is starkly divided politically, and the secular culture sees anyone with opposing views as morally deficient and unworthy of the same treatment that they are entitled to. The combination of these two trends—disdain for religious views and severe political division—has produced a series of problems for the church.

The most serious problem is that the church, which consists of sincere Democrats and Republicans, has become divided by political disagreements instead of being united in our common love for Christ. Another issue is that Christians of both political factions lack the knowledge that will help them to understand the other side's perspective and, more importantly, prevent them from seeing the biblical errors in their own perspectives. Members of the church have gone along with lies that keep them in the good graces of their political and social groups rather than embracing the truth that keeps them in right standing with God. The Bible says that God's people are destroyed for a lack of knowledge (Hosea 4:6), and what is happening to the church in today's society is a clear illustration of that.

From a cultural standpoint, the division and moral decline makes America susceptible to losing its position as the freest nation in the world and becoming a tyrannical country. Many people have written books warning about the rise of tyranny in our society. I reference some of these books, and I add to their insights in hopes of giving you a more comprehensive understanding about the issues we face in our country, and I do this as someone who has seen this battle from different angles. I have a unique vantage point. I am a fairly young Christian constitutional lawyer who also happens to be a black woman. I've worked in education, law, politics, and the media. I believe the Lord has compelled me to share what I've learned in the hope of building up the church and strengthening our country. I hope that reading *Uncommon Courage* inspires you to become a warrior for Christ in a hostile culture in need of God's love.

PART 1

THE FOUNDATION
FOR FREEDOM

CHAPTER 1

CHRISTIANITY AND THE CONSTITUTION

The good news of Jesus Christ is the news of eternal freedom. The old covenant was one of bondage because we were slaves to a law that we could not obey (Hebrews 8:7-13). There was a never-ending cycle of death to atone for our inevitable sins. Then God offered Jesus Christ as the final sacrifice. God's Son was the only one who could perpetually atone for us, providing release from the bondage of sin and eternal freedom from our spiritual debt. As the apostle Paul said, "It is for freedom that Christ has set us free. Stand firm, then, and do not let yourselves be burdened again by a yoke of slavery" (Galatians 5:1).

Not only does God give us spiritual freedom, He also gives us the freedom to choose whether we want to accept that gift. Despite the possibility that we might reject Him, God still grants us the choice, even though He could undoubtedly force us to obey Him. The gift of free will is one of God's greatest acts of love toward us. God loves us enough to let us choose, and it is all the more

satisfying to Him when we choose to love Him by our own voli-
tion. In this way, God is not a tyrant. He is a loving ruler who,
though uncompromising in His standards and unchanging in His
ways, allows us to walk according to our own will. He is a righteous Father who gives us free will, while also openly inviting us
to experience true spiritual freedom by walking in righteousness
with Christ. Our God models true leadership.

As Christians, we often take our spiritual freedom for granted
and bind ourselves again to sin by allowing our bodies and carnal
minds to have mastery over us. Scripture says the human heart is
inherently wicked (Jeremiah 17:9), which is why the Holy Spirit
must constantly work within us to refine our behavior and trans-
form us to become more like Christ. Over time, we can become
slack about disciplining ourselves because God perpetually for-
gives us, and we sometimes face no immediate earthly consequences for our actions.

Much like we are inclined to take our spiritual freedom for
granted, we often take our cultural freedom for granted. The
right to choose and exercise our Christianity in a free society
tends to produce a lukewarm, complacent church. This is analo-
gous to a believer who takes the compassion and grace of God for
granted and, over time, becomes halfhearted in his or her quest
for sanctification.

Freedom is a central principle of Christianity, and that principle thrives in a culture that embraces the freedom of religion.
That is, the freedom to choose Christ over all other gods among
us. This is one reason a Christian foundation was essential for
the national freedom that Americans possess now. To ensure that
America was a bastion of liberty, the founders needed to give

everyone the freedom to choose their own religious path. This is why a national ruler must never seek more authority over us than God exercises over us. Any nation that chooses to be "under God" must acknowledge that freedom of religion is essential to truly being under Him.

> *Freedom is a central principle of Christianity, and that principle thrives in a culture that embraces the freedom of religion.*

While we know that the church can and often does thrive in a culture where Christianity is persecuted, there is no question that a culture that freely allows Christianity is beneficial to the church. A church that is not punished by the government for acting and speaking according to biblical truths can be effective in spreading the gospel, serving the local community, and discipling believers.

Historically, this is why totalitarian regimes always begin their reign of persecution by stifling the speech and assembly of the religious population. Those who believe in a higher authority cannot be easily tamed by tyrannical government because they resist the idea that the government is supreme. Thus, a tyrant must rid his nation of the devout.

A tyrant is anyone who seeks to intercept our relationship with God by usurping His position in our lives. As we seek to obey God, we are coerced to obey the government, and we are penalized if we don't. To establish an obedient, loyal population of subjects, a tyrannical government must train everyone to consider the government their supreme authority, or their god. This is why tyrannical systems of government are contrary to Christianity and the church should oppose governments that exercise such power.

Communism is tyrannical because it aims to be the supreme authority in its citizens' lives. The threat of tyrannical government should awaken the complacent within the church and embolden a lackluster democratic society.

A BIBLICAL VIEW OF GOVERNMENT

God's original design for government was one in which people were subject only to Him. "For kingship belongs to the Lord, and he rules over the nations" (Psalm 22:28 ESV; see also 1 Samuel 12:12). But to ensure that justice prevailed, God appointed judges. During this period of time there were 14 judges, including Samuel (1 Samuel 7:15-17). Then the Israelites approached Samuel and demanded a king instead. When Samuel approached God about the people's demand, God told Samuel to grant the request because "they have not rejected you, but they have rejected me from being king over them" (1 Samuel 8:7 ESV).

Samuel tried warning the Israelites that a king would become a tyrant. A king would collect a tenth of their wages (verses 15, 17) and help himself to their sons, daughters, and flocks (verse 11-18). The people's ability to serve God would diminish because they would be forced to be slaves to the king. Yet the Israelites disregarded the warning and, because they wanted to be like all the other nations (1 Samuel 8:19-20), they insisted that Samuel give them a king. As a result, Samuel was the last of Israel's judges.

Samuel anointed Saul as the first king of Israel (1 Samuel 10:1). Saul was chosen because he was a righteous man who, at first, obeyed God. But it didn't take long for Saul to succumb to the corrupting nature of power, abandon God's guidance, and become a tyrant over Israel (1 Samuel 12–16).

While God allowed His people to be ruled by kings, He wanted kings who submitted to Him and would rule under His direction. But this proved difficult. As fallen humans, even the kings who yielded to Him made poor decisions and let their stature and power give them inflated egos. The kings who failed to submit to Him ended up usurping His role among the people. These kings sought power and exaltation, indulged in sin, and subjugated the righteous.

Even Solomon, the man whom the Bible calls the wisest of all the kings, failed to maintain his allegiance to God. Though God prohibited kings from marrying many wives or becoming greedy (Deuteronomy 17:16-17), Solomon violated these requirements despite his wisdom (1 Kings 11:1-8). This demonstrates that even those of us who are committed to God are susceptible to letting our power overcome us and deteriorate our allegiance to God.

These biblical examples illustrate a principle at work in government: absolute power corrupts absolutely. By nature, we are prideful, arrogant, and self-centered, and when we have too much power over others, these traits are exacerbated. Power can make us want to be a god over others, which is a satanic sentiment.

The Bible highlights a powerful truth: Man is evil without God, and sometimes even with God. We are constantly thinking of ourselves, and, under the right conditions, we will seek to control others. This Christian understanding about the nature of men provides the basis for the structure for America's government and our national Constitution. Both are designed to limit the amount of power given to one person or to a small group of people. It is by design that, in America, the greatest amount of power rests in the hands of the American people.

HUMAN NATURE AND GOVERNMENT

The Founding Fathers' religious convictions informed the way they structured the American government. For one, most of them possessed a deep faith in God. Benjamin Franklin and Thomas Jefferson believed in God later in life, but ultimately, they both had foundational beliefs about the nature of man that resembled the teachings of Christianity.[1] Most of the Founding Fathers believed in the deity of Jesus Christ.[2] Because of the cultural beliefs and expectations at the time, all the Founding Fathers were students of the Bible and considered it authoritative, and all—except Jefferson—considered the Bible to be the inspired Word of God.[3]

A Christian worldview about Jesus Christ and the Bible births a specific worldview about the nature of human beings: Given the opportunity, people will abuse power and become tyrants. Such a view naturally leads to the belief that any system of government must, in some ways, tame the evil inclinations of the human heart.

This stands in contrast with those who believe that people are generally kindhearted and trustworthy. An idealistic view of human nature is most in line with socialist or Communist governments. This perspective states there is little need to restrict the power of government rulers because the assumption is that rulers can manage their power responsibly.[4]

We know that the Founding Fathers believed that God revealed

His moral standards for human behavior through the Bible.[5] They believed that His moral standards should be translated into human laws that ensured people would conform to God's will for society.[6] God's standards reveal that we have certain natural rights, and His standards demand that those rights are respected by others.

It's clear that people will violate God's standards when given the opportunity, especially if there are no penalties for their actions. This puts people in the position of relying on the government to enact laws and enforce them for the protection of society. This is often referred to as social contract theory: People will agree to live under governmental authority so that the government can protect the rights of the people. Essentially, we give up some control of our lives to the government so we can gain the protection that only the government can provide. We cede power to the government to help secure our rights, yet the government is entitled to possess only the power that the people—and God—delegate to it.[7] But it is one thing for everyone to agree that we need a government; it is quite another to create a government that everyone agrees on.

CREATING THE CONSTITUTION

By the time America's founders explored the prospect of a constitution, they had learned many lessons regarding government power. Great Britain's government was too powerful, and Americans went to war to be freed from the crushing authority of the monarchy.[8] But after the American Revolution, the new country erected a soft, almost powerless government under the Articles of Confederation. This caused chaos and anarchy, and the newly freed nation nearly collapsed as a result.[9]

The creators of the new government would have to walk a tightrope to formulate a government with enough power to bring order to society but not enough power to allow tyranny.[10] Ultimately, the founders came up with a system that would divide powers into three distinct but equal branches of government and between the federal and state governments. This structure was designed to prevent the country from ever being subject to only one person or a small group of people who had the power to create, interpret, and enforce laws.[11]

The US Constitution consists of three main parts: the preamble, seven articles, and 27 amendments. The preamble begins and ends with "We the People of the United States…do ordain and establish this Constitution for the United States of America." The articles explain the framework of the government and define the scope of power for each branch and between the states and the federal government. For example, Article I explains the structure of the legislature, how members of the House and Senate are chosen, and lists the specific powers of Congress and its limits. Article II describes the executive branch. Article III describes the judicial branch. Articles IV-VII focus on the powers of the states.

The process to amend the Constitution is extensive, and of the thousands of amendments that have been proposed, only 27 have become law. A national amendment requires three-fourths of the states to ratify, or approve, it. The first ten amendments are called the Bill of Rights. These were proposed together and are focused primarily on an acknowledgment of the rights of the people. They spell out the various rights of the American people, including freedoms of religion, speech, and association; the right to remain silent; the right to be free from illegal search and seizure; protection from excessive bail and cruel and unusual punishment; and more.

BIG IDEAS OF THE CONSTITUTION

Protecting Individual Rights

As the Declaration of Independence declares, "That to secure these rights, Governments are instituted among Men." The principal purpose of the Constitution is to protect individual inherent rights, and the commitment to protecting those rights has a theological foundation. Even Thomas Jefferson, who most people would argue was the least religious of all the founders, said, "God who gave us life, gave us liberty at the same time. Can the liberties of a nation be secure when we have removed their only sure basis, a conviction in the minds of the people that those liberties are the gift of God?"[12]

The belief that we are made in God's image means that we are all inherently worthy. He loves us equally and sees us equally (Genesis 1:26-27; 9:6). God is not a respecter of persons (Acts 10:34); thus, His view of justice commands equality under the law (Exodus 23:6-7). This is the core reason that caste systems are unbiblical and cannot be justified with a Christian view of the world, even though many people have tried to do so.

The opposing view of humanity relies on an evolutionary foundation. It presupposes that evolution created inequalities in humans' abilities, intellects, and ultimately, their worth. Some people are stronger, faster, and smarter; therefore, they should be granted special and superior treatment in society over those who have not supremely evolved. The Nazis and white supremacists have relied on this evolutionary humanist view to promote their propaganda.[13]

Contrary to the supremacist view of the world, God demands that we are all treated with equal respect, and ultimately, that we do not interfere with His authority in another's life. God's commandments create protection for our individual rights. His demand that we do not kill (Exodus 20:13), enslave (Exodus 21:16; Deuteronomy 24:7), or steal (Exodus 20:15) protects our rights to life, liberty, and property.[14]

Speaking of slavery, we have not yet examined the stain on the Constitution of the Three-Fifths Compromise and the passage of the subsequent Thirteenth Amendment. We will. For now, try to embrace the fact that the general principles that laid the foundation for the Constitution were sound and based on the idea of freedom, even if the founders violated those principles in provisions designed to protect the immoral institution of slavery and ultimately, the idol of greed. Later in the book, we will see that it was these Christianity-inspired foundational principles that ultimately led to the eradication of slavery and the end of Jim Crow.

But generally, remember that the Constitution's acknowledgment of and promise to protect our God-bestowed rights are found primarily in the Constitution's amendments, especially the Bill of Rights. These amendments lay out specific rights that the government must not infringe upon, and the Twenty-Seventh Amendment states that the rights listed are not exhaustive.

When you review some of the world's tyrannical governments, you can quickly determine which rights you would want for protection against such a system. You'd want a government that couldn't tell you who to worship, what to say, or who you can associate with. You'd want a government that couldn't lock you up without a fair trial or enter your home and search it without a warrant. You'd want the right to protect yourself and your family. You'd want to be free—that is, not a slave to a person or the government. The Constitution's amendments protect all these rights.

Limitations on Concentrated Power

To ensure our inherent rights are protected from government interference and control, our Constitution establishes a limited government with limited power. Contained primarily in its articles, the Constitution divides power among different branches of government and between the federal government and the states. Each are designated with distinct powers that prevent one branch or the state or federal government from controlling the people. The branches of government consist of the executive, legislative, and judicial branches. In essence, this design splits the power of a "monarchy" into three different roles.

The legislative branch consists of Congress and the state legislators; each enacts laws for the respective populations. Historically, this is the branch that was supposed to be the most powerful because it had the authority to decide what would be legal in society. Every representative or senator is elected by the people, and the people trust that those who are elected will vote for the laws that reflect the desires of the constituents. This is the branch we should scrutinize the most, although that rarely happens because the other two tend to hold our attention more.

The executive branch, which consists of the office of the president, its federal agencies, and the state governors' offices, are charged with enforcing the laws. We tend to grant this branch more attention because of the influential role of a president or governor. This branch often reflects the regal influence of the monarchy.

The judicial branch includes the federal and state courts, and its job is to interpret the laws enacted by the legislators. It presides over criminal and civil disputes and weighs the facts against the laws and decides the appropriate outcome of conflicts. The role of the court is corrective, not creative. The court's job is not to change the law or decide what the law should be. Its role is to use the law to decide the outcome. Over the last few decades, the courts have drifted from the founders' design for them—they have issued decisions that functionally have the force of law. This has produced tense political conflicts around the nomination of judges, particularly to the US Supreme Court.

In addition, both the states and the federal governments have specific powers. Generally, the federal government has the power to control commerce, levy taxes, control the military, and declare war. The states' powers focus on policing, including the safety, health, and welfare of citizens. This includes the power to control education, to have state courts, and to have a state criminal justice system. The federal and state governments are considered separate sovereigns, and the federal government cannot force the states to uphold federal laws.

A fundamental aspect of the separation of powers is the checks and balances between them. Each branch of government has the power to correct the other. For example, if the legislature enacts a law that violates the Constitution, the court can strike down that law. But, if the court makes an incorrect decision, the legislature can make a law to overturn that decision and nullify it.

This separation of powers is one of America's biggest barriers to tyranny. This is why Americans must guard closely the distribution of power and ensure that no branch or sovereignty is usurping the power of another. For example, we must ensure that the judicial branch is not making laws, or that the federal government is not overreaching and inappropriately controlling the states. When any branch of government or sovereign violates the separation of powers doctrine, it should be called out and immediately corrected through the proper channels available in our laws.

A Republic, Not a Pure Democracy

America is not a pure democracy. A pure democracy is one in which the majority rules. In a republic, the people elect representatives to make decisions on their behalf. A republic seeks to provide all populations with some authority over the direction of the country, even when they may represent only a small subset of the population. As John Adams said, "The very definition of a Republic is 'an Empire of Laws and not of Men.'"[15]

Congress consists of two houses. In the House of Representatives, the states are assigned representatives according to their respective populations. States with more people have more representatives. But the Senate provides equal representation to all the states. Each state gets two senators, no matter what its population. For any law to be passed on the entire country, both houses of Congress must vote for it. This ensures a balance of power between the bigger states and the smaller.

A republic is focused on protecting individual rights regardless of whether the majority of people agree with those rights. There are many instances in which the majority will support the suppression of the rights of others because they dislike a group of people. The power of a republic is in its ability to uphold its laws in the face of a changing culture.

The Electoral College provides a clear illustration of this principle.

The Electoral College is how the Constitution ensures that states with the largest populations, like California or Texas, do not alone control the outcome of a nationwide presidential election. Each state gets a certain number of electoral votes, and then the Electoral College representatives for that state choose the president. Despite the fact that a state like North Dakota may not be nearly as powerful in its populace as California, each state still has a say in choosing the president.

This may seem obvious by now, but this difference between a republic and a democracy is also paralleled in the differences in our political parties. Democrats tend to focus more on social and community impact. They tend to believe that laws should evolve with the needs of the people. The more people tend to lean in the direction of a new social idea, the more the Democratic party pushes for the advancement of that idea. It's not exactly accurate to say that the Democrats represent the majority view, but instead, that they often represent the cultural trends.

Republicans are grounded in tradition and history and resist adjusting laws based on social expectations. Republicans want to protect core individual rights with as much respect to the original intention of those rights as possible. Democrats believe individual rights are not absolute, especially in the face of a changing culture. There are pros and cons to both approaches, and they both need the other to find the proper balance.

IS THE CONSTITUTION OUTDATED?

One of the major criticisms about the Constitution is that it is too old to be relevant. Ironically, this same criticism is aimed at the

Bible. Recall that it was biblical principles that provided the foundation for much of the Constitution and its structure. The idea that people are inherently inclined to abuse power inspired the separation of powers and is designed to protect people from tyrannical behavior. No one is exempt from this expectation of abuse of power. Everyone is capable, and thus no one can be trusted. In addition, all of us are made in the image of God, and God commands that we respect His commandments in our treatment of one another.

The Constitution's allowance for slavery is the most valid criticism against it, and this would be a good time to address this issue. We will explore this several times throughout this book, but as a starting point, let's explore how the founders integrated slavery into the Constitution.

The founders generally understood that Congress would have the most power of all the branches of government because it would have the authority to enact laws. Because of this, the most contentious arguments between the delegates were about state representation and voting in Congress.

In relation to representation, the lesser-populated states wanted to ensure that they had as many votes as more-populated states to prevent the latter from dominating the country. The more-populated states argued the opposite: that voting in Congress should be proportional to the states' populations.[16] This resulted in two houses of Congress: the House of Representatives and the Senate. Each state would be assigned representatives in the House according to population, but in the Senate, each state would have two senators. This was known as the Great Compromise, and it also included a decision on a contentious issue that still has ramifications today: slavery.

Because representatives in the House would be apportioned based on population, the delegates needed to decide whether slaves would count as people. Of course, the South wanted slaves to be counted as people for representation purposes, but this also meant that the Southern states' taxes would be higher because taxes were also calculated by population.[17]

Founding Father James Wilson suggested that the delegates adopt a rule that became known as the Three-Fifths Compromise. Under this rule, representation would be according to the whole number of white and free citizens, but all others (except Indians not paying taxes) would be counted as three-fifths of a person.

The Three-Fifths Compromise haunts the integrity of the founders and the Constitution to this day. While the principles that influenced the Constitution are timeless, the document is not infallible.

But we need to understand our history in order to learn from it. That means we must understand that just because the Founding Fathers didn't always do the right thing doesn't mean that they didn't know what was right. This is one of the reasons that CRT ideology is so problematic. You cannot learn the truth from lies. Thus, we should commit to teaching students the full picture of America's founding, including its Christian roots. It should be a regular exercise in pedagogical methods for students to evaluate whether the country's leaders and citizens are living up to those basic Christian principles.

While we know that the motivations for slavery were greed and pride, it is necessary to acknowledge the motivations for its ultimate abolition too. As an article published in *National Affairs* noted:

The point of axioms, however, is that their truth doesn't depend on whether we acknowledge or respect them. They are statements about the nature of reality. And the Declaration recurs to the language of natural law: A "Supreme Judge of the world" stands as the final governor of humanity. His divine edifice contains fixed truths that men can ascertain even when their observance (as with the slaveholding founders) falls short. Laws given by men should, accordingly, conform to those given by nature and nature's God.[18]

ALWAYS RELEVANT

Many people's eyes glaze over when someone starts talking about the Constitution. And I want everyone to realize how dangerous that is. It's not that the document should be part of our everyday conversation, but we need to know it. We need to understand it. We cannot protect it if we don't. It's also true that those who criticize government must have a thorough understanding of how it works in order to present workable solutions towards its perfection.

The Constitution is a contract that specifies how much power the government is allowed to exercise over us. That means we feel its impact every day. We should aim to understand a document that so persistently impacts our lives. But we often take it for granted because we cannot perceive losing the freedom that the Constitution promises. The next chapter will show us what happens when the government doesn't make or keep those promises.

CHAPTER 2

THE ROADMAP
TO TYRANNY

George Orwell was a man on a mission to warn the world about tyranny. But despite his goal to fight against an authoritarian system, his name became synonymous with the system he despised. The term *Orwellian* describes tyrannical government action, reminiscent of the chilling dictatorship in a novel we'll explore in this chapter—*Nineteen Eighty-Four*, a story that readers do not easily forget.

In Oceania, a province in the fictional Airstrip One (formerly Great Britain), telescreens cover the landscape, buildings, and every residence. The screens are filled with images of Big Brother, the ruling Party's leader and the only public face of the government. Behind those repetitive, brainwashing images are ever-watchful eyes that monitor everything people do and say. Oceania's ruling ideology is IngSoc, short for English Socialism, and everyone is required to blindly commit to this ideology or face severe punishment for contrary behavior, speech, and even thoughts, called "thoughtcrime."

The book's protagonist, Winston Smith, is a low-ranking employee of the government. He stews in discontent over the government's oppression, especially in his job at the Ministry of Truth, which manipulates the news, entertainment, and education so that they all communicate the ruling Party's ideology. Winston's job is to rewrite historical records to comport with Big Brother's agenda.

Besides the Ministry of Truth, which is in charge of propagating lies, Oceania's other "ministries" serve equally contradictory purposes. The Ministry of Peace perpetuates war, the Ministry of Love tortures dissident citizens, and the Ministry of Plenty ensures that the people of Oceania remain in a state of perpetual lack and starvation. The Party's reliance on linguistic incongruity is displayed in its slogan: War is Peace, Freedom is Slavery, and Ignorance is Strength.

The Party requires total devotion and, consequently, anything that might threaten a person's allegiance to the Party is illegal, including history, facts, freedom, and love. Anyone who rejects the Party becomes an "unperson," and all evidence of their existence is destroyed.

Despite the threat of torture, Winston secretly vents his revolutionary thoughtcrimes in a diary, which he purchased illegally in protest of the State's suppression of its citizens' individuality. Every day, Winston stews with hatred for the Party. In the course of doing his job, he falls in love with a fellow rebel and coworker, Julia. They meet for romantic trysts, paranoid that the Party will eventually discover their illegal devotion to each other.

Eventually, Winston and Julia connect with a fellow dissident, O'Brien, who is the leader of a secret revolutionary group, the Brotherhood. Winston and Julia join the Brotherhood, glad to have found others who are likeminded. But, during one of their meetings, officers storm in and arrest everyone. Winston is separated from Julia and imprisoned, and eventually he learns that O'Brien was actually a member of the Party's Thought Police.

At the Ministry of Love, O'Brien tortures and brainwashes Winston, coercing him to pledge his allegiance to the Party. But Winston resists despite the ferocious nature of the punishment. Winston's obstinance results in O'Brien resorting to a most vicious tactic.

The Party turns to Winston's biggest fear—rats, a fear that the Party discovered because of its continuous surveillance of its citizens. O'Brien straps Winston to a chair and secures a cage full of rats to Winston's head and waits for the rats to eat Winston's face. The Party will force Winston to be devoted only to the Party by destroying his love for all others. In pain as the rats begin to gnaw on his face, Winston breaks and begs O'Brien to release him and to take Julia instead.

At the end of the novel, Winston and Julia indifferently pass each other on the street. They no longer love one another. They are devoted only to Big Brother.

If you've never read *Nineteen Eighty-Four*, the story is so chilling that you leave the book relieved that it is fiction. But at the time that Orwell wrote the book, the tyrannical regimes of the real world were far more sinister than the fictional depiction in the novel. In fact, there are many who believe that Orwell wrote *Nineteen Eighty-Four* as a commentary on Nazism and Stalinism.

Winston's defeat is a poignant warning about our own vulnerability amid the pressure of an all-powerful state. You might wonder whether you would resist such oppression. Why didn't the people of Germany or the Soviet Union resist their tyrannical leaders? Surely some of them did, but why did so many succumb? What kind of people allow the establishment of an oppressive and murderous regime? The surprising answer is that ordinary people like you and me are responsible for the development of tyranny.

WHEN THE SOIL IS RIPE FOR TYRANNY

While many people know about the widespread oppression that took place in Germany and the Soviet Union and currently takes place in Venezuela, China, and elsewhere, most are unaware about how such systems develop. Like Orwell, other key individuals through-out history have answered the call to warn the world about tyranny. In 1951, Hannah Arendt published *The Origins of Totalitarianism*, outlining how specific conditions prepared the culture for Nazism and Stalinism to take root. She wrote, "Totalitarianism has discov-ered a means of dominating and terrorizing human beings from within."[1] Later, in 2000, *BBC*'s documentary "Five Steps to Tyr-anny" offered another warning.[2] In it, Sheena McDonald referred to historical accounts, academic experiments, and social psychol-ogy to evaluate how people are gradually inoculated to live under oppressive dictatorships.

These works, and my own observations about history, will serve as a basis for the three steps I propose here—steps that place coun-tries on the path to tyranny. I will summarize the steps and add to them a biblical perspective about why tyrannical tactics can be effective on so many people. Neither the *BBC* documentary nor Arendt's book discuss how our inherently wicked desires can be preyed upon by the government, but as Christians who realize that all people are sinners, it's important for us to understand why this is so, and never underestimate our own vulnerability. Taken together, the messages in Arendt's book and the *BBC* documentary are clear and compelling: Tyranny is made possible by ordinary people like you and me.

Step One: Divide and Isolate

The first step to establishing a tyrannical regime is to divide the people. One tactic is to fuel supremacy by creating feelings of superiority in one group and feelings of inferiority in an underclass. The government uses the resulting differences, no matter how subtle, to divide the population and build a culture of "us versus them." It is surprisingly easy to create underdogs in a society, and often, our personal desire to be better than others can be exploited by leaders for their own ends.

The *BBC* documentary presented an experiment carried out by an elementary school teacher, Jane Elliot. The day after Dr. Martin Luther King Jr. was assassinated, Elliot led her all-white third graders through an experiment that taught them how ugly and easy prejudice really is. Elliot divided the class by making rules that separated the brown- and blue-eyed children in the room. She told the students that the two eye colors couldn't play together. She said that blue-eyed people were superior in intelligence and physical appearance, and thus, that they were superior in classroom status. Brown-eyed children couldn't use the same bathroom or drinking fountain as the blue-eyed. By the end of Elliott's experiment, the brown-eyed children were despondent, depressed, and angry, while the blue-eyed children grew more vicious by the day. In one memorable moment, a brown-eyed child was crying and complaining about a blue-eyed child who pointed at him and called him "brown-eyed."

Division causes people to isolate from one another and, as Arendt argues, it produces loneliness and social atomization, which, in turn, helps fuel a totalitarian society.[3] When people are more isolated and anxious, they become more susceptible to deceptive leaders who promise peace and unity but are really seeking to impose control over people.[4]

A Divided Body

In the Bible, the first story of division appears in Genesis, when Satan divided Adam and Eve from God and from each other. Satan, appearing as a serpent, persuaded Eve to disobey God by making her doubt what God had said. He asked Eve, "Did God really say, 'You must not eat from any tree in the garden'?" (Genesis 3:1). Eve replied, "We may eat fruit from the trees in the garden, but God did say, 'You must not eat fruit from the tree that is in the middle of the garden, and you must not touch it, or you will die'" (verses 2-3).

Now, Eve responded with what she thought God said, although inaccurately, for she added, "You must not touch it." Satan pivoted quickly, telling her, "You will not certainly die" (verse 4). He convinced her to eat, enticing her with the idea that when she did so, she would "be like God" (verse 5). Adam also eats the fruit.

Afterward, God came strolling through the garden, and Adam and Eve, knowing they were in trouble, hid from the Lord. When God called for Adam, Adam confessed his sin, but blamed it on Eve (verses 8-12). The rest, as we say, is history.

In one encounter, Satan interrupted Adam and Eve's fellowship with God *and* created disharmony between the couple. This serves as a model for how Satan succeeds in deceiving people today. He divides us from God, and then he divides us from each other.

The Power of Unity

Another story in Genesis demonstrates the power of unity. In chapter 11, we read the story of the Tower of Babel. At the time, the whole world was united in language and speech, and the people decided to build a tower that would reach the heavens because they wanted to make a name for themselves.

In response, the Lord said, "If as one people speaking the same language they have begun to do this, then nothing they plan to do will be impossible for them. Come, let us go down and confuse their language so they will not understand each other" (Genesis 11:6-7). Here, God was acknowledging that even when people were not submitting to Him, if they were united, nothing would be impossible for them. The opposite is also true: People who are divided will not accomplish much.

Step Two: Sear the Conscience

After dividing its people, a tyrannical regime will capitalize on several human tendencies with the goal of searing the consciences of individuals so that they are more submissive and more easily manipulated.

First, humans have a surprising tendency to follow orders, especially from those who are in positions of authority. One experiment featured in the *BBC* documentary revealed that 50 percent of people will comply when asked to give up their seats on public transit. One hundred percent will cooperate if the person asking is accompanied by someone in a uniform, even if that uniformed figure never says a word. People acted even before being given any good reason to comply.

Second, people can be conditioned to obey orders even to the point of inflicting oppression and pain on another person. One of the most famous experiments demonstrating this horrifying phenomenon was conducted at Yale University by Stanley Milgram. The experiment required participants to administer a painful electric shock whenever a student gave a wrong answer to a question. Astoundingly, even though some of the participants questioned the utility of the experiment, if the experiment leader pressured the participant, they would continue shocking the student, despite cries from the student that he or she was in unbearable pain.

The documentary notes that such conditioning begins with an ideology. In the case of the electric shock experiment, the ideology was "we want to help learning." Then the leader assigned roles to various people, with some being made supervisors and others appointed as underlings. Those in supervisory positions were pushed to carry out astonishingly vicious actions when their leader asked them to start with small steps and gradually increase the danger level. In the electric shock experiment, the "teachers" started by giving 15 volts of shock and were pushed to deliver a 45-volt shock to the "students." Apparently, people felt less responsible for their immoral or harmful actions if they could blame them on an authoritarian mandate.

Because of this, as *BBC* proclaims, "The mindless, blindly obedient are the real threat to society."[5] Such mindlessness creates a rabid obsession to the prescribed ideology—an obsession that produces disdain for any information that contradicts that ideology, regardless of how factually accurate the information is. Note this passage in *Nineteen Eighty-Four*:

> Applied to a Party member, it means a loyal willingness to
> say that black is white when Party discipline demands this.

> But it means also the ability to believe that black is white, and more, to know that black is white, and to forget that one has ever believed the contrary. This demands a continuous alteration of the past, made possible by the system of thought which really embraces all the rest, and which is known in Newspeak as doublethink. Doublethink is basically the power of holding two contradictory beliefs in one's mind simultaneously and accepting both of them.[6]

Arendt confirmed this phenomenon when she explained how totalitarian regimes inject their populations with propaganda and the willingness to believe convenient lies.[7] In totalitarian states, people are willing to accept "monstrous forgeries in histography" to bolster their arguments about the hated groups. The silence in the face of lies also induces us to tolerate immoral rules, especially when those immoral rules target the "others."

As a result of tyranny's reliance on lies, tyranny cannot allow voiced opposition, and thus, it cannot tolerate free expression. Tyrants must create an illusion, and free speech has the power to break that illusion as well as trigger the consciences of the listeners. Thus, silent bystanders are an essential ingredient to maintaining tyranny.

The real lesson here is that united groups of people with an intact moral compass have power. Tyrants and their inner circles are usually small in number, which means they need public compliance to stay in power. On their own, they are no match for the population they seek to control. The silver lining is that the same tribal instinct that might inflame people toward division (a tolerance of lies) and to embrace an immoral government may also persuade them to fight for the truths felt deep in the conscience.

Step Three: Exterminate

The final step of tyranny is extermination. To fully understand this step, it's important to recognize that at the core of every person's psychology is the tendency to do evil acts. This lines up with what the Bible says about humanity—in Genesis 8:21, the Lord says that "every inclination of the human heart is evil from childhood." Understanding this truth will keep us from assuming that any superior sense of morality we might have is enough to keep us from willingly subjecting ourselves to the whims of a dictator.

The Rwandan Genocide

One memorable example of this is the Rwandan genocide that took place in 1994. In the early 1900s, Belgian colonists arrived in Rwanda and classified the Rwandan people according to their tribes, giving them identity cards that corresponded to their tribal background. The Belgians exalted the Tutsis above the Hutus and, as a result, the Tutsis enjoyed supremacy in society, with better jobs and educational opportunities.

Unsurprisingly, after decades of oppression, the Hutus rioted in 1959. Some 20,000 Tutsis were killed, and others fled to neighboring African countries. In 1962, when Rwanda gained its independence from Belgium, the Hutus rose to power and their resentment against the Tutsis caused the Tutsis to be blamed for every problem in society. Eventually, the Rwandan radio airwaves came under government control, and the majority tribe, the Hutus, saw this as an opportunity to broadcast disparaging and hateful messages about the Tutsis.

A combination of political unrest and the formation of competing political parties produced tensions that culminated in the killing of a political leader honored by the Hutus. Although no one could pinpoint the killer who shot down the leader's plane, the Hutus blamed the Tutsis and began slaughtering them. Having already primed the population with anti-Tutsi propaganda, the Hutus publicly murdered Tutsis without reservation.

The killings spread quickly throughout the country. Anyone who resisted was killed, and others either quickly fell silent or actively participated. The government-sponsored radio messages revealed where hiding Tutsis could be found and incited ordinary Hutus citizens to murder their neighbors.

Over a period of 100 days, 800,000 people were killed.

For the most part, the Rwandan genocide happened in full view of the world, with few discussing it and none intervening. By the time the United Nations finally sent troops to Rwanda to bring a stop to the slaughter, the genocide was over.

China's Social Credit System and Reeducation Camps

China provides a modern example of a more nuanced form of ideological extermination. Human Rights Watch describes China as "a one-party authoritarian state that systemically curbs fundamental rights."[8] The US State Department warned that "the People's Republic of China is an authoritarian state in which the Chinese Communist Party [CCP] is the paramount authority."[9]

China's social credit system monitors people continuously from multiple sources. At every moment all across the country, millions of cameras with facial-recognition technology silently record and assess people's behavior. The CCP also closely monitors things like government records, business transactions, financial documents, education records, smartphone activity, internet usage, and behavior.

In China, one key aspect of the social credit system is that neighbors are expected to "watch" each other. In this way, the CCP is able to guarantee its perpetual surveillance goals. As the US State Department says, the system is calculated to promote self-censorship and incentivizes citizens to police each other.[10] Because a person's social credit score measures his loyalty to the government, and because the government is constantly on the lookout for dissidents and rewards loyalty, there is great temptation for citizens to become a government informer.

The Chinese government also closely surveils the activities of Christians, Muslims, the Falun Gong, and other religious groups. According to the US State Department, more than one million Uyghurs and other Muslims have been imprisoned in camps designed to "erase religious and ethnic identities."[11] But members of all faiths are routinely questioned by the government and often imprisoned. Freedom House reports that at least 100 million Protestant Christians, Tibetan Buddhists, Uyghur Muslims, and Falun Gong practitioners face very high levels of persecution.[12] In the Uyghur detention camps, officials have abused, tortured, and killed as many as 20,000 detainees, according to the Uyghur Human Rights Project. Despite international laws that ban torture, the practice persists.[13]

Like all government forms of control, China's social ranking system conditions people to be loyal to the government and not each other. These systems force people to compete with one another because they are constantly ranked above or below others. Unfortunately, it's fairly easy for the government to turn people against one another. Sometimes it happens without the government's initiation. The point is that division makes our country vulnerable because it can be used by power-hungry leaders to gain illegitimate power.

SOFT TOTALITARIANISM IN AMERICA

America is marching steadily toward tyranny. The easiest step for most of us to recognize is the increasing cultural division that is present in the US today. In a 2019 article, Thomas Carothers and Andrew O'Donohue discuss the "especially multifaceted" political polarization in America. According to Carothers and O'Donohue, a "powerful alignment of ideology, race, and religion renders America's divisions unusually encompassing and profound." A unique characteristic of US polarization is the combination of race, ideology, and religion within each political party—what the author calls the "iron triangle" of US polarization.[14]

Over the past few decades, our two-party system has created a stark line between those on either side. We tend to stereotype each political party based on race, religion, and socioeconomic status. For example, most blacks and other minorities are assumed to be Democrats, which causes minorities who are Republicans to face ridicule, be ostracized, and insulted for not conforming to those expectations, regardless of their reasons for not doing so.

On the other end, many people assume that Republicans are mostly white and that they don't care about racial oppression.

Because of the radical, inhumane torture and enslavement of blacks in pre-Civil War America, and the subsequent era of cruel oppression after emancipation, there still remains a tension between races. As a result, Republicans and Democrats are often at odds because of the ways they approach matters involving racial conflict. These disparate perspectives continue to produce tension between the races and within the races.

Moreover, while Democrats perceive Republicans to be morally deficient for their alleged discounting of racial oppression, Republicans express similar moral judgment toward Democrats for their celebration of abortion and their rejection of biblical perspectives on the family and sexuality. Many Republicans often use these issues as reasons to say the Republican party is the correct party for Christians, leading to much consternation among Christians who are Democrats.

These conflicts and many people's almost-rabid commitment to their respective party's beliefs are likely contributing to a more widespread callous indifference to some modern-day evil practices. The most obvious example is abortion, including those in which violent dismemberment takes place. Even self-proclaimed Christians attempt to justify this practice, and this, in turn, contributes to dividing the church.

To some extent, both the American people and the Christian church have abandoned their divine identity and submitted themselves to secular ideologies. We have become a people under desire, fully surrendered to our physical appetites and ready to punish anyone who stands in the way. We'll discuss these ideas more later in the book, but for now, suffice it to say that these general examples demonstrate that America's conscience has been seared to an unrecognizable degree.

While nothing quite as extreme as the extermination that took place in Rwanda exists in America now, we do face a soft form of totalitarianism that, given time, could quickly lead to the hard or more severe, violent form. Rod Dreher writes in *Live Not by Lies* that America is on the precipice of soft totalitarianism. His description of this new, modern form of totalitarianism is that it is not established through "hard" means like armed revolution, at least initially. Rather, the modern kind of totalitarianism masks its hatred of dissenters under the guise of helping and healing.[15]

Dreher explains that "soft totalitarianism exploits decadent modern man's preference for personal pleasure over principles, including political liberties." According to Dreher, the public will support, or at least not oppose, the coming soft totalitarianism because it will be satisfied and placated by hedonistic comforts, or our fleshly desires.[16] Consequently, he posits, a progressive anti-Christian militancy is steadily overtaking society. This contempt for Christian principles is evident in the calls to dethrone Christian perspectives from politics, education, family life, and even Christianity itself. Such a move of ideological extermination is one we cannot hope to resist without strengthening our individual spiritual lives and doctrinal unity within the church.

AN OPPORTUNITY FOR THE CHURCH

Now that we have surveyed real-life illustrations of how countries end up on the road to tyranny, it should be clear why any of us are capable of submitting to tyranny, given the right conditions. Tim Radford, who wrote an article for *The Guardian* about the *BBC* documentary, said, "Tyrannies happen because ordinary people are surprisingly willing to do tyranny's dirty work."[17] Most important for the Christian to understand is that the tyrant manipulates our propensity to sin for the purpose of producing the desired results. Remember that tyranny needs an obedient majority to do its bidding.

This means that we must become knowledgeable about the types of conditions that prime people to nurture tyranny in their midst. When we see ourselves taking the first steps down the road to tyranny, we must do what we can to take action and change course immediately.

In order to have such an impact on our country, the church must be united in its purpose. The apostle Paul discussed the importance of unity at length in the book of 1 Corinthians. He said, "I appeal to you, brothers and sisters, in the name of our Lord Jesus Christ, that all of you agree with one another in what you say and that there be no divisions among you, but that you be perfectly united in mind and thought" (1 Corinthians 1:10). Remember God's words about what happens when people are united: nothing will be impossible for them.

The church must be the barrier to unjust and tyrannical government in our society. We are meant to be salt and light in the world, and when we do our job, we can be the personification of God's moral compass, modeling for the world how people should treat one another and boldly opposing oppression.

We are meant to be salt and light in the world, and when we do our job, we can be the personification of God's moral compass, modeling for the world how people should treat one another and boldly opposing oppression.

Not only can the church provide a spiritual roadblock to tyranny in America, we have a legal one as well. One of America's strongest legal obstacles to tyranny is the US Constitution. The forefathers were cognizant of man's inherent flaws. They knew that humans are inclined to exalt themselves above others, obey authority even when it's wrong to do so, and that equal treatment must be demanded rather than requested. Of course, history tells us that our forefathers were themselves flawed and we know that their own greed and power were on display in the drafting of some of the Constitution's provisions. But the foundational principles of the document, the principles that allowed us to correct mistakes like slavery, are sound and are the biggest obstacle to any person or group that wants to change America's foundation for freedom. In other words, in order to advance tyranny in America or infuse tyrannical principles, it is necessary to erode the legal mechanisms written in the Constitution—or at the very least, to take steps to ensure those protections will not be honored.

This is why it is so important for us to educate ourselves about how our laws protect us from the establishment of tyranny. It is very possible for the abolition of freedom to take place in America too. We are no different from the people in other nations who have succumbed to dictatorships in the past or present. But for those of us in the church, there is a fine balancing act to walk. We are meant to live as responsible citizens, and our rights do, in fact, permit us to have an active role in pushing back on tyranny. Yet it is also important to understand that Scripture calls us to reform hearts, not governments. However, as we reform the hearts of men with the proclamation of the truth, we can also influence the culture and the government for the advancement of God's kingdom.

A CONSCIENCE
CONTRARY TO TYRANNY

A t the religious liberty law firm I worked for, First Liberty
Institute, the president and chief counsel, Kelly Shack-
elford, speaks to the summer interns about the importance of religious liberty. He illustrates his apt point by making the
interns watch an episode of *The Twilight Zone* called "The Obsolete Man," which originally aired in 1961.

The episode begins with a chillingly apropos opening narrative:

> You walk into this room at your own risk, because it leads
> to the future, not a future that will be, but one that might
> be. This is not a new world; it is simply an extension of
> what began in the old one. It has patterned itself after
> every dictator who has ever planted the ripping imprint
> of a boot on the pages of history since the beginning of
> time. It has refinements, technological advances, and
> a more sophisticated approach to the destruction of
> human freedom. But like every one of the super-states

that preceded it, it has one iron rule: logic is an enemy
and truth is a menace. This is Mr. Romney Wordsworth,
in his last forty-eight hours on Earth. He's a citizen of
the State but will soon have to be eliminated, because
he's built out of flesh and because he has a mind. Mr.
Romney Wordsworth, who will draw his last breaths
in The Twilight Zone.

Wordsworth, a librarian, enters a shadowy courtroom. Jurors stand
on both sides, robotic and expressionless. Wordsworth approaches
the chancellor, the presiding judge over Wordsworth's crimes. The
state has been eradicating books; thus, Wordsworth's chosen profession is viewed as worthy of extermination. The chancellor questions Wordsworth and declares that because of his profession and
his intolerable belief in God, Wordsworth is "obsolete" and should
be sentenced to death. Before his sentence, Wordsworth retorts, "I
am nothing more than a reminder to you that you cannot destroy
truth by burning pages."[1]

The state graciously allows Wordsworth to choose his form of
execution and, in fact, will televise it to the citizens of the state
mostly because showing executions of defectors produces more
obedient citizens. As the chancellor reveals, "It's not unusual that
we televise executions. It has an educative effect on the population."[2]

Wordsworth requests his manner of death be kept secret and
that he die in his home. The chancellor agrees, and he also accepts
Wordsworth's request that the chancellor visit Wordsworth in the
last hour of his life.

The home is cozy and filled with books. In full view of the state,
Wordsworth informs the chancellor that his chosen manner of

execution is a bomb set to go off in 30 minutes. Wordsworth reveals that he has bolted the door, and that the chancellor cannot get out. Being careful not to show his panic, the chancellor sits and smokes a cigarette while Wordsworth pulls out a Bible and says, "It's been hidden here for over twenty years. It's a crime punishable by death, so it's the only possession that I have that has any value at all to me."[3]

Over the next 30 minutes, Wordsworth reads aloud Psalms 23 and 59, speaking of the Lord as his Shepherd and that a fool says in his heart, "There is no God." The chancellor grows increasingly anxious and, finally, when there is only a minute left until the bomb's detonation, he begins to beg to be let out of the home. In desperation, the chancellor declares, "In the name of God, let me out." Wordsworth unbolts the door and the chancellor runs out seconds before the bomb explodes. Wordsworth dies with a smile.

In the next scene, the chancellor is at the mercy of the same court he once led. Because of his intolerable weakness and declaration of God, the court also deems him obsolete, and he is beaten to death by his former colleagues.

The narrator concludes the show by stating,

> The chancellor, the late chancellor, was only partly correct. He was obsolete. But so is the State, the entity he worshipped. Any state, any entity, any ideology which fails to recognize the worth, the dignity, the rights of Man...that state is obsolete. A case to be filed under "M" for "Mankind" in The Twilight Zone.

This episode gives me chills. While the dystopian nature of this scene seems far from reality, it is, in fact, a version of many realities that have existed and still do exist. In the pages to come, we will survey the greatest totalitarian nations in history, in which crueler and more violent versions of this *Twilight Zone* episode existed. They all illustrate a similar message as this episode: Tyranny cannot tolerate religion.

THE TYRANT DESTROYS THE CONSCIENCE

To control the minds of people, a tyrant must sear their consciences so that they will accept the government's immoral actions. To do that, a tyrant must begin by squelching the moral voice of the culture: the religious. A tyrant cannot condone a divinely committed population because they will actively resist the tyrant's edicts in full view of the rest of the nation, influencing others to also resist. The religious will denounce the tyrant's immorality. Thus, their opposition is a threat to his autocracy. The commitment of the religious to obey God in the face of injustice is a threat to anyone who wishes to command the minds of the people and possess their complete allegiance. Therefore, for the tyrant, the religious must go.

The tactics for destroying the religious vary, depending on the culture. As we saw in the previous chapter, any culture can eventually slide into violent behavior, but even without physically annihilating the religious, there are other ways to nullify their impact.

Historically, religious persecution has been violent and overt, but over time, oppressive governments have discovered new and subtle ways to accomplish their ends. Let's review some of the world's tyrannical regimes and see what we can learn from them.

THE EVOLUTION OF TYRANNY

In 2019, Marion Smith wrote for the *Wall Street Journal*:

> Most faiths call their adherents to look up past the things of this world. In communism, this world is all there is—a world of productivity and material goods, but nothing else. Thus, the regimes that rule in its name seek to destroy the soul and deny any freedom of conscience. Faith, hope, charity and forbearance are dangerous ideas for a system that relies on fear and envy. And what is dangerous must be destroyed. To create the communist heaven on earth, the faithful must abandon their beliefs or endure a living hell.[4]

Smith makes the point that Communism's hatred of religion "is a feature, not a fault," and that "communism is not only irreligious but anti religious." Karl Marx said so as well. In fact, Marx begins *The Communist Manifesto* by saying, "Communism begins where atheism begins." The strategy for building an atheistic government starts with stifling and punishing religious exercise.

The Soviet Union

The second leader of the Soviet Union, Joseph Stalin, enforced "militant atheism."[5] In October 1917, after the Russian Revolution, the Soviet Union became the first state to have an official objective to eliminate religion. During this primitive form of Communism, the government subjugated the population with brute force, which included killing people who resisted.

But the Soviet government used some manipulative tactics to

woo, rather than force, the population into submission. Within just weeks of the revolution, the Soviet Union established the People's Commissariat for Enlightenment to remove all references to religion from school curriculums. Under Khrushchev, it became illegal to teach religion to your own children.[6]

In the years that followed, churches and monasteries were destroyed or reappropriated to things ranging from public toilets to propaganda museums. While Russian Orthodox adherents were the target because of their large numbers, believers in Protestant denominations, Islam, and Judaism were also persecuted.[7] In 1917, there were more than 50,000 houses of worship, but by 1939, only about 500 remained open.[8] Between 1917 and 1921, the Soviet Union killed 300 Orthodox clergy.[9] Scholar Todd M. Johnson estimates that Soviet authorities killed 15 million Christians in prison camps between 1921 and 1950 and another 5 million over the next 30 years.[10]

Nazi Germany

Nazi Germany imposed a more sophisticated form of Communism that marked an evolution from physical force to brainwashing. The persecution of religious people in Nazi Germany, the most infamous tyrannical state of all time, is well documented, mostly due to the Nuremberg war-crimes trials conducted in 1945 and 1946.[11] In what the Nuremberg prosecutors called a "criminal conspiracy," a group of Nazis, which included Adolf Hitler and his propaganda minister, Joseph Goebbels, planned the gradual annihilation of the Christian church using lies and manipulation. The prosecutors' documents reveal that the plan to annihilate the religious was established before the Nazi rise to power.[12]

One of the Nazi government's tactics included forming alliances with churches to use their social power to accomplish the Nazi's own purposes. Most notable was a 1933 contract between the Nazis and the Roman Catholic Church. Hitler offered financial incentives for the church in exchange for "a pledge of loyalty by the clergy to the Reich government and a promise that Catholic religious instruction would emphasize the patriotic duties of the Christian citizen."[13] Hitler kept these alliances intact until he assumed full dictatorship and then immediately violated the agreements that had been made with the churches.[14]

By 1937, the relationships soured completely. Pope Pius XI criticized the Nazi regime in public letters to all the Catholic churches, and Pastor Martin Niemoller condemned the state's control over the Protestant churches. Niemoller was eventually sent to a concentration camp for his dissent. Religious groups' written critiques of the Nazis were confiscated, and eventually the churches resorted to reading the letters to the congregants during services. Notably, in response to consistent dissent, the Nazis arrested 700 Protestant pastors.[15]

To avoid the inconvenience of the courts, which often acquitted the religious leaders arrested by the Nazis, the Nazis eventually declared that anyone who said anything injurious to the Nazi government would be deprived of court review and ruthlessly punished by "protective custody"—that is, in concentration camps.[16]

Meanwhile, Hitler and other members of the Nazi party publicly declared that they were Christians, but this was just another way of deceiving the people. In one speech in 1928, Hitler said, "We tolerate no one in our ranks who attacks the ideas of Christianity...in fact our movement is Christian."[17]

But Joseph Goebbels, Hitler's propaganda minister, stated

that there was an "insoluble opposition" between Nazism and Christianity.[18] He wrote in a diary entry in 1939 that Hitler "passionately reject[ed] any thought of religion."[19] And Otto Strasser, Hitler's confidant, wrote in his 1940 book *Hitler and I*, "Hitler is an atheist."[20]

More specifically, Hitler and other Nazi leaders believed in Germanic racial superiority.[21] In a 2014 debate between Cardinal George Pell and Richard Dawkins, both men agreed that Hitler was a staunch believer in social Darwinism.[22] So, despite Hitler's deceptive rhetoric claiming Christianity, Hitler ultimately believed in achieving a level of social and political control where he was subject to no one but himself.

The demands of the national Reich Church further demonstrate the true authoritarian intentions of Hitler's government, despite cloaking those intentions in religious rhetoric. His government called for exclusive right and control over all churches and the immediate termination of publishing, disseminating, or displaying of the Bible. All church altars were called to post nothing but *Mein Kampf*, Hitler's manifesto.[23] In a 1941 speech, US President Franklin D. Roosevelt declared Hitler's plan to eradicate all religion from Germany:

> Your Government has in its possession another document, made in Germany by Hitler's Government…It is a plan to abolish all existing religions—Catholic, Protestant, Mohammedan, Hindu, Buddhist, and Jewish alike. The property of all churches will be seized by the Reich and its puppets. The cross and all other symbols of religion are to be forbidden. The clergy are to be forever

liquidated, silenced under penalty of the concentration camps, where even now so many fearless men are being tortured because they have placed God above Hitler.[24]

For Hitler, Christianity was a religion for slaves. He despised its ethics and ideals of meekness and conscience and believed it violated Darwinism's law of natural selection and the survival of the fittest.[25] But Hitler's hatred for Christianity does not compare to the way in which he hated the Jewish people.

Keeping to his beliefs in natural selection, Hitler despised the Jewish people because he believed that they were biologically inferior to Germans. Hitler identified the Aryan as the "genius" race and the Jew as the "parasite." He believed it was necessary for the German people to preserve the purity of the Aryan race and ensure the elimination of the Jewish race, which he stated "must necessarily be a bloody process."[26]

In 1933, the Jewish community was less than 1 percent of the total population in Germany. Capitalizing on their minority status, Hitler began to relentlessly slaughter the Jews.[27] Through the suppression of moral objections, slow and methodical propaganda designed to sear the consciences of the people, and detention and violent treatment of any defectors, Hitler and his Nazi regime murdered more than six million Jewish people.

China and the New Persecution

Since its founding, the People's Republic of China has heavily persecuted its religious residents. Its goal is to eradicate any thought or act that contradicts the goals of the state. *The Wall Street Journal* reported that the Chinese government arrests, imprisons, and kills religious adherents like Tibetan Buddhist monks. And others, like the Falun Gong, have their organs forcibly removed for the benefit of government officials. All churches must agree to preach state-approved messages and the Chinese Communist Party (CCP) currently approves the selection of bishops and priests.[28]

From 2018 to 2021, between 5,000 to 10,000 Christians were arrested, and many Protestant clergy were sentenced to prison for long periods of time.[29] In 2021, *Foreign Policy* estimated that nearly two-thirds of Protestant churches were underground.[30] The government regularly collects reports that track worshippers. In some churches, crosses were taken down and depictions of Jesus or Mary were replaced with portraits of President Xi.[31] The government demands that churches install cameras so the CCP can monitor worshippers' actions and pastors' messages.[32]

But China's treatment of the Muslim Uyghurs is the most brutal. *The Wall Street Journal* reported that as many as three million members of this group have been forcibly imprisoned in "re-education camps" in the providence of Xinjiang. The government brainwashes them to create mindless, committed residents who will easily succumb to the demands of the government. Those who are released are reportedly placed in forced labor camps and continuously brainwashed and controlled.[33]

Notably, China's governing leaders studied the fall of the Soviet Union intensely and know that both Catholicism and the Protestant faith contributed to the collapse of Communism in Eastern Europe.[34] As a result, the Chinese government modified its approach to Communism to embrace more deceptive, subtle practices of control.

Cameron Hildith for *National Review* noted:

The CCP has learned that the long-term survival of a Communist super-state is better served by managing domestic elements hostile to Communist ideology rather than attempting to abolish them outright. Wild horses might drag the people of China away from their tyrannical government, but rather than shoot the horses in true Soviet style, the CCP has decided to break and bridle them instead. The new Chinese Communism is one of social control, not social revolution. And so its architects allow for just enough capitalism to keep themselves in power, and for just enough Jesus to keep out Christ.[35]

In 2020, the Chinese Communist Party produced a state-approved Bible. One example of the changes includes a new depiction of the woman caught in adultery (John 8:3-11). In the correct version, Jesus releases the woman and tells her to sin no more. In the CCP version, Jesus stones the woman to death and says, "I too am a sinner. But if the law could only be executed by men without blemish, the law would be dead."[36]

While in some ways the oppression of religion in an authoritarian state has become more subtle over time, as China demonstrates, the goal is still the same. That is to create a submissive population that the government can control without opposition, no matter how immoral or oppressive the government's actions become.

This new soft totalitarianism, as Rod Dreher calls it, is still just as dangerous as the old Soviet Union way. Dreher argues that China demonstrates that it is possible for a modern and wealthy society to be totalitarian. The CCP is controlling a nation of 1.4 billion people and creating one of the most sophisticated tyrannical societies in history.[37]

THE THREAT TO RELIGIOUS
FREEDOM IN AMERICA

This is a good reminder that freedom of religion is the cornerstone freedom. Once the government destroys that, all other rights come toppling down. Once the governments we've reviewed were able to interfere with the religious conscience of the people, they then attacked freedom of speech, association, due process, and so on.

While America's founding documents were set up to prevent Communism and tyrannical government, we should not take our protection from such autocracy for granted. Many modern-day fascist regimes have governing documents that promise their citizens basic freedoms, including China. Unfortunately, these documents mean nothing if they are not strictly guarded and enforced. And the same is true for our Constitution. Because freedom of conscience is the cornerstone right, we should guard this freedom fearlessly.

One of the primary reasons America sought its freedom from Great Britain was to rid itself of the established Church of England. This is why the Founders mention religious freedom right from the start in the First Amendment. The First Amendment of the US Constitution begins, "Congress shall make no laws respecting an establishment of religion, or prohibiting the free exercise thereof[.]" This statement, known as the Religion Clauses, consists of both the Establishment Clause and the Free Exercise Clause. Jurists and scholars consistently debate the exact scope of the religious liberty protected by the First Amendment. But, at a minimum, it prohibits Congress from, in the words of James Madison, compelling "men to worship God in any manner contrary to their conscience."[38]

The Establishment Clause was originally intended to do exactly what it implies: prevent the government from establishing an official church and demand that its citizens worship there. The Free Exercise Clause means the government cannot interfere with your ability to worship God according to your conscience. These might seem simple, but, as with most aspects of the law, we rely on the courts' interpretations to truly understand what these rights currently mean in America.

With the rise of Marxist ideology and secular humanism in America, we have seen direct attacks on the right to religious freedom. This is in part due to the mistakes that some among the religious population made during slavery and the civil rights movement in endorsing racial superiority. Many have used these major missteps by the church to attack religious liberty protection in its entirety. For example, you may have heard the media calling religion a "guise for discrimination."[39] We will unpack this further in the next chapter, but for now, I'll say that just because some religious people endorsed horrible practices, and in some cases, invoked their religion to do it, it does not mean the solution is to destroy the right to religious freedom. Doing so would inevitably destroy all other basic rights, which would impact everyone, not just the religious.

While the culture has become increasingly antagonistic toward those who disagree with current popular ideology, this was not always so. For example, in 1993, Congress overwhelming passed an important bill called the Religious Freedom Restoration Act (RFRA), designed to overturn a Supreme Court decision, *Employment Division v. Smith*, that gave the government the power to restrict religious exercise without much justification. RFRA overturned the application of *Smith* on the federal level and reimposed, by statute, the rules that formerly applied to federal religious liberty claims prior to *Smith*. Liberal and conservative groups and politicians of both parties united on the measure. RFRA passed the Senate 97-3. It passed the House of Representatives *unanimously*. It was fully supported by the American Civil Liberties Union (ACLU).

But fast-forward two decades later, and you can hardly recognize the political landscape. RFRA is heavily targeted by Democrats. Measures like the Equality Act, Do No Harm Act, and others aim to nullify the protections in RFRA. The ACLU now opposes the legislation.

The primary reason for this political shift is the growing schism between those who support the culture's changing views on sexuality and those who do not. The religious Americans who believe that only men and women should be married are at odds with the prevailing orthodoxy. Growing numbers of politicians claim to have changed their minds or have been forced to abandon their positions for fear of being accused of bigotry.

For example, Democratic Representative Jerrold Nadler backed RFRA in 1993, but in 2019, he was a co-sponsor of the Equality Act as chairman of the House Judiciary Committee. He stated in a hearing, "Religion is no excuse for discrimination in the public sphere, as we have long recognized when it comes to race, color, sex, and national origin, and it should not be an excuse when it comes to sexual orientation or gender identity."[40]

You should immediately notice Nadler's comparison between racial supremacists and those who disagree with same-sex relationships. In *Obergefell v. Hodges*, the decision that legalized same-sex marriage, Justice Samuel Alito prophesied that this comparison would be "exploited by those who are determined to stamp out every vestige of dissent."[41] Comparing religious believers with those who agreed with racial supremacy produces a radical demonization of the religious population that persists even when the conflict does not involve sexuality. This comparison is the primary threat to religious freedom today.

In other cases involving religious displays or private religious practices, government officials have attempted to banish those displays or practices in the name of "the separation of church and state." This phrase, which was originally written by Thomas Jefferson to declare that the government should not interfere with church affairs,[42] is now being used to demand that religion be banned from the public arena entirely. One example is the case of a WWI memorial that was challenged as an Establishment Clause violation because it was in the form of a cross.[43] In this case, one of the lower courts even suggested cutting the arms off the 100-year-old monument in order to avoid offending people.

Another example is the case of Joseph Kennedy, a high school football coach who was fired for saying a brief, silent private prayer on the field after the games. The school district in that case argued that it could censor Coach Kennedy's private prayer because they should protect the students from seeing him engaging in the practice.[44] This is particularly disturbing when you consider that many of the same people who do not believe in public religious practices or displays also argue for children in school to view sexually explicit materials.

This perverted view of the Establishment Clause produced a watered-down version of the Free Exercise Clause and fueled government hostility toward religious practice, such as in the case of Coach Kennedy. Other cases were about states that offered financial benefits for parents, schools, or other entities, but refused to allow the religious to qualify for that same benefit.[45]

This growing intolerance for religion is setting the stage for the destruction of the legal protections for religious individuals and for the country to begin a slippery slope towards tyrannical government. In a 2020 speech for the Federalist Society, US Supreme Court Justice Samuel Alito said that "religious liberty is slowly becoming a disfavored right."[46]

THE CHURCH MUST PROTECT RELIGIOUS FREEDOM

A weak church creates a vulnerable nation. Remember that a tyrant's goal in getting rid of religious adherents is to get rid of anyone who will convince the rest of the population to disobey the oppressive government. Thus, as a tyrant silences believers, he will also slowly destroy the conscience of the people.

A weak church creates a vulnerable nation.

Ultimately, the worldview that all men are made in the image of God and that we possess rights beyond the reach of man is the foundation for our right to religious liberty. The right to live according to your conscience is the most deeply personal right you can have. Religious convictions that include the inherent worth and rights of man are a direct affront to a tyrannical government, which is why most nations that fall into tyranny often embrace a secular humanist and Darwinian worldview. Distancing the people from theism primes the population to tolerate the oppression of the religious and eventually the oppression of everyone.

And America is growing less religious. Gallup estimates that an increasing number of Americans express no religious preference. Over the past two decades, the percentage of Americans who do not identify with any religion has grown from 8 percent in 1998–2000 to 13 percent in 2008–2010 and 21 percent from 2018 to 2021. The membership of houses of worship is strongly linked to age. About 66 percent of US adults born before 1946 belong to a church, compared with 58 percent of baby boomers, 50 percent of adults in Generation X, and 36 percent of millennials. The limited data on church membership for the adult members of Generation Z are so far showing church membership rates similar to those for millennials. For the first time in eight decades, the majority of the population are not members of houses of worship.[47] It is likely this trend will continue, which means it is even more important for the religious to fight to protect religious freedom in America. The further in the minority we become, the more vulnerable we will be.

One of the counterarguments I repeatedly hear from Christians is whether it is biblical to fight back against the government. Should we turn the other cheek and just do what we're told, even when we believe the government is wrong?

This question was especially salient during the COVID-19 health crisis, when many states and local governments targeted churches for disparate treatment, allowing places like private offices, liquor stores, casinos, and even strip clubs to stay open, while prohibiting corporate worship. These tactics were legally and morally wrong.

For example, in April 2020, On Fire Christian Church in Louisville, Kentucky, decided to hold drive-in Sunday services for its attendees. This would allow members to congregate and feel a semblance of fellowship but remain safe from transmitting the coronavirus to one another. Despite the fact the plan posed no risk of transmission, the mayor of Louisville prohibited all Easter gatherings, including drive-in church services.

Now, let's set aside the fact that the mayor's mandate specifically targeted a religious holiday, being that he issued it the week of Easter. Still, his proclamation reveals the truth about the corruptive nature of power we've examined several times in this book. The mayor used the health crisis to overstep his power and overtly discriminate against a religious group during a sacred holiday.

On Good Friday, First Liberty Institute filed an emergency injunction asking a federal court to declare the mayor's prohibition unconstitutional and allow the church to gather on Easter. District Court Judge Justin Walker issued the first legal victory for churches concerning COVID restrictions. And he issued his decision the evening before Easter:

> On Holy Thursday, an American mayor criminalized the communal celebration of Easter. That sentence is one that this Court never expected to see outside the pages of a dystopian novel, or perhaps the pages of The Onion. But two days ago, citing the need for social distancing during the current pandemic, Louisville's Mayor Greg Fischer ordered Christians not to attend Sunday services, even if they remained in their cars to worship—and even though it's Easter. The Mayor's decision is stunning. And it is, "beyond all reason," unconstitutional.[48]

Judge Walker's order blocked the mayor's mandate and permitted Christians to worship on Easter. This win set the stage for other victories regarding restrictions against religious worship and provided a lens by which other courts would closely examine the exercise of governmental power in an emergency.

That victory led to victories for other churches in places like Mississippi, New York, and DC. Eventually, the US Supreme Court ruled 5-4 in *The Diocese of Brooklyn v. Cuomo* in favor of New York's houses of worship, stating:

> But even in a pandemic, the Constitution cannot be put away or forgotten. The restrictions at issue here, by effectively barring many from attending religious services, strike at the very heart of the First Amendment's guarantee of religious liberty.[49]

A situation like a global health crisis will force us to reexamine the balance between protecting the safety of the public and checking authoritarian power. Very few things in America thrust this balance into the spotlight like governments' responses to COVID-19. And many Christians struggled with knowing when to obey the government and when to practice civil disobedience. Like many of life's tough questions, the answer is found in Christianity's sole written authority: the Bible.

There are dozens of examples of civil disobedience in the Bible. Many of the people were forced to disobey the commandments of tyrant kings rather than disobey God. The first instance of civil disobedience is depicted in the story of the Hebrew midwives who defied the king of Egypt's order to kill all the Hebrew male babies.

"The midwives feared God; they did not do as the king of Egypt commanded them, but they let the boys live" (Exodus 1:17 NRSV).

Nebuchadnezzar was the longest-reigning king of Babylon from 605 BC to 562 BC. He was a fierce tyrant who demanded total allegiance from his subjects. He rejected God, rebuilt pagan temples, and destroyed the temple of Solomon. In Daniel 3, Nebuchadnezzar created a golden idol and commanded the people to worship and bow before it. Shadrach, Meshach, and Abednego refused, and were put into a fiery furnace as punishment (Daniel 3:1-23). The Lord rescued the three men in a miraculous situation worth reading, but for now, suffice it to say that Nabuchadnezzar was not willing to tolerate religious convictions that threatened his desire for absolute power. Yet these three men were willing to risk their lives to disobey him.

In Daniel 6, King Darius issued an edict that no one could pray to anyone but him for a period of 30 days. Daniel brazenly defied the edict by praying to the Lord...with his window wide open. As a result, King Darius cast him into a lions' den (Daniel 6:1-23). The Lord rescued Daniel, just as He rescued the three Hebrew men from the fiery furnace.

And of course, the disciples' belief in Jesus Christ's deity led them to disobey the government and religious rulers. In Acts 4, the leaders prohibited John and Peter from preaching the gospel, but they kept speaking, and were eventually thrown into prison.

In one of the most compelling stories of civil disobedience, the Sanhedrin flogged the disciples for preaching the gospel. The Bible says that afterward, the "apostles left the Sanhedrin, rejoicing because they had been counted worthy of suffering disgrace for the Name. Day after day, in the temple courts and from house to house, they never stopped teaching and proclaiming the good news that Jesus is the Messiah" (Acts 5:40-42). This isn't just civil disobedience. This is outright rejoicing in the act!

While it is true that Romans 13:1 says, "Let everyone be subject to the governing authorities, for there is no authority except that which God has established. The authorities that exist have been established by God," Paul never meant for us to obey the government over God. He certainly did not do that. He was beaten, imprisoned, and suffered greatly because he would not obey the government's mandates to stop preaching about Jesus (Acts 16:22; 27–28; 2 Corinthians 11:16–12:10).

We must keep in mind that the persecution of the church is not necessarily a bad thing for the church. While it is individually difficult, it tends to produce a fervent, growing body of Christ. For example, China's Christian population is one of the fastest growing in the world. The Council on Foreign Relations cited a 2018 estimate from Purdue's Center on Religion and Chinese Society, which states that there are between 93 million to 115 million Protestants in China.[50] Much of this growth has happened since 2010, and some projections propose that by 2030, China could exceed America and have the largest population of Christians in the world.[51]

MIND YOUR CONSCIENCE

Ultimately, we actively oppose oppressive governments because they are contrary to Christianity. A tyrannical government wants to be supreme and will not accept people exalting anything above it, including God. It will only tolerate a submissive, mindless citizen. If that citizen's rights of conscience, speech, press, or the like interferes with the government's objectives, the rights must yield to the state. This is fundamentally contrary to God's will for any of us.

At the same time, we must also recognize that oppressive principles like Communism take hold of the culture because there is a desire within the population to correct wrongs like racism, classism, and criminal injustice. Communists can captivate the culture with promises, no matter how deceptive, that a totalitarian government can cure these societal ills. The church would do well to adopt the persuasive, powerful, and fervent nature of some of these tyrants, but do it to further the gospel. Historically, the church has been quiet when it comes to some of America's most abhorrent actions. In part, this is because we have allowed our environments to sear our consciences, and it has produced a callous indifference within us that has allowed the world to use us for its benefit. And ultimately, that has made us futile and, in some cases, detrimental for God's kingdom.

Today, in America, popular culture expresses disgust and intolerance for theology, moral absolutes, and dissent. Anyone who threatens the power of the culture is deemed obsolete. In such an environment, how do we keep our consciences? How do we know when our freedoms are being threatened? We will explore the answers to these questions in the next section.

PART 2

KEEPING YOUR CONSCIENCE

CHAPTER 4

FEAR GOD

When I was a corps member in Teach For America, I shared my testimony in a small group of twentysomethings who were mostly secular-minded, nonreligious people. It sparked a discussion about whether the culture could maintain a moral compass without a religious or theistic foundation. The reactions were mixed, but to my surprise, most people acknowledged that the culture was unlikely to maintain a strong moral compass without a foundational belief in God.

God's Word provides an unchanging foundation for us. If there is no foundation, there is no standard. Once we unravel a basic standard of morality and declare that everyone can set their own moral code, it becomes impossible to maintain consistent societal agreement about what is right and wrong. This is why the culture's current promotion for personal truths is so problematic. Truth can be found, explained, experienced, and even debated, but it cannot be created. Truth exists outside of us.

We live in a culture that wants to destroy moral absolutes. The problem is that the culture promotes moral relativism as compassion. It is this false framing of compassion that deceives many, especially Christians. This often happens because we don't know God's viewpoint on the subject, and we don't know enough of God's Word to deduce a biblical conclusion if the explicit answer is absent in His Word. Once the culture begins to loosen our grip on God's foundation, it begins to reprogram us to accept and defend immoral viewpoints because we believe that it is the compassionate thing to do. This destroys our moral compass and puts us in the same mindset as the worldly, secular society.

In *Live Not by Lies*, Rod Dreher discusses the profoundly anti-Christian militancy that is steadily taking over society, one described by Pope Benedict XVI as a "whole wide dictatorship of seemingly humanistic ideologies," which is the manifestation of "the spiritual power of the Antichrist."[1] This humanistic viewpoint is prevalent in academia, corporate institutions, education, and more increasingly, in government and the law. Anyone who doesn't bow to it is ostracized or labeled antiquated, bigoted, or anti-whatever. Similarly, during Communism in the Soviet Union, artists and intellectuals alike advocated for Communist ideology and openly detested and mocked religion. This public movement toward humanism and Communism started almost two decades before actual Communism took over.[2] Humanism usually begins in the culture and eventually branches off into the government so that it can begin to coerce and outright force people to adopts its views.

Romans 13 tells us that "every person is to be in subjection to the governing authorities. For there is no authority except from God, and those which exist are established by God...Therefore it is necessary to be in subjection, not only because of wrath, but also for conscience's sake" (verses 1, 5 NASB 1995). This means we must obey the laws so that our consciences are clear before God. But we must be careful not to subject ourselves to government authorities or rules that attempt to usurp God's role in our lives. To make this distinction, our consciences must be able to differentiate between proper and improper roles of government, much like the biblical believers we learned about in the previous chapter.

Our hearts are wicked and are inclined to believe and act in ways that please the flesh (Jeremiah 17:9). Therefore, we must keep reminding ourselves of the truth in order to continue living by it. To do this, we must stay in godly community and diligently read the Word. The world is persuasive, and it is constantly bombarding us with its positions. To combat this barrage of lies effectively, we must hold Scripture as the final authoritative answer on every subject, and to do that, we must know Scripture. Dr. Tony Evans says in his book *Kingdom Politics*, "[E]very question facing us today has two answers: God's answer and everyone else's. And when those two differ, everyone else is wrong."[3]

To stand firm in a hostile and deceptive culture, you must keep your conscience. This means you must maintain a biblical stance on all societal issues regardless of the shifting cultural trends. To succeed against the constant barrage of deceit, you must know biblical truth, and you must have knowledge of the relevant subjects when they arise. The foundation of keeping your conscience begins with knowing and accepting who God is and who God says you are.

REVERENCE: KNOWING WHO GOD IS

Reverence means that we worship and respect who God is. We accept His decisions, and we obey His standards. Accepting who God is and allowing Him to hold the authoritative position in our life is true reverence, and it is the most important aspect of our conscience to protect. This is obeying the first commandment: "Thou shalt love the Lord thy God with all thy heart, and with all thy soul, and with all thy mind" (Matthew 22:37 KJV).

Accepting who God is and allowing Him to hold the authoritative position in our life is true reverence, and it is the most important aspect of our conscience to protect.

We are likely incapable of truly understanding the vastness of who God is. But the Bible provides a framework that gives us some understanding. According to the Bible, God is omnipresent (Psalm 139:1-10) and omniscient (1 John 3:20). God is spirit (John 4:24), and He is love (1 John 4:8, 16). He is the way, the truth, and the life (John 14:6). He created all things (Colossians 1:16). He is the Alpha and Omega (Revelation 22:13), meaning He is the beginning and end of all creation. He is justice (Deuteronomy 32:4; Psalm 50:6). He is the Word (John 1:1, 14) and He does not lie (Numbers 23:19). He makes all things possible (Matthew 19:26). God is light, and in Him there is no darkness at all (1 John 1:5). His ways and thoughts are higher than ours (Isaiah 55:8-9). He is our Wonderful Counselor, Prince of Peace, Mighty

God, Everlasting Father (Isaiah 9:6). He does not change (Malachi 3:6; Hebrews 13:8). He does not faint or grow weary; His understanding is unsearchable (Isaiah 40:28). God is a consuming fire, and He is jealous for us (Deuteronomy 4:24). He will be with us wherever we go (Joshua 1:8-9; Psalm 139:4-10). His way is perfect (Psalm 18:30). God is all-knowing (Psalm 139:2-4). He is all-powerful (Jeremiah 32:17). There is none like God (2 Samuel 7:22).

The culture will try to convince us that our freedom depends on our ability to do what we want when we want. But Christians must know that true freedom is living within biblically mandated restrictions. Tony Evans presents a comprehensive definition of freedom that needs no adjustments. He defines biblical freedom as "the unimpeded opportunity and responsibility to choose righteously, justly, and legally regarding one's divinely created reason for being."[4] God wants you to be free to maximize your gifts and talents in order to benefit His kingdom.

We often get the misguided impression that living according to God's expectations is restrictive, but in fact, living in God's will is the freest way to live because only He knows the optimum path for you. What most people misunderstand is that, even if you are living according to what you perceive to be your own desires, you are actually in bondage. That is, you are in bondage to your ever-changing, unpredictable, ignorant emotions. Or, as the Bible says, you are a slave to sin (Romans 6:20). And you are in bondage to society's principles, which are not intended to produce good works from you, but rather, are designed to control you.

Remember that all tyrannical regimes get rid of religious doctrine because God's definition of freedom requires that we are able to legally live out His will for our lives, which means God intends for the government's power to be limited. He expects the government to regulate you for your safety and for societal protection, but it is supposed to operate with as little power over you as possible. Ultimately, God expects His doctrines to be in control, which requires that we live within certain boundaries.

When I taught elementary school, I spent the first two weeks of school building classroom culture. My goal was to set behavioral standards for the rest of the school year. We spent the first week talking about the kind of classroom the students wanted to learn in. I asked them if they thought a classroom with no rules would be enjoyable. They unanimously said no. Even at ten and eleven years old, the students knew that a classroom with no rules would leave them vulnerable to mistreatment from other classmates and would produce a classroom where I cannot teach, and they cannot learn. As the governing authority of the class, my job was to keep them safe and create an environment where they could learn. I walked the students through this process because I wanted them to internalize why rules are important and why they should follow them. And the more well-behaved my class was, the more freedom I could give them.

In order for us to truly experience the freedom God desires for us, we must accept His standards and expectations for us. We must also hold the government accountable to adhere to its role in society. Just like I needed to be there to enforce the classroom rules to protect my students from a classmate's misbehavior, the government must guard society against those who move outside the bounds of civilized behavior. Ultimately, this concept rests on the truth that our hearts are wicked, and we will likely act up if we are not held to a standard. This is the foundational understanding for accepting God's sovereign role in our lives and maintaining reverence for Him in our conscience.

In Exodus 20, the Lord speaks to Moses on Mount Sinai and gives him the covenant law in the form of stone tablets, also known as the Ten Commandments (verses 1-17). Meanwhile, Aaron is babysitting the Israelites, and they begin to get restless without Moses. They eventually ask Aaron for something to worship (Exodus 32:1). To appease the people, Aaron asks them to give him gold, and he melts the gold into a golden calf—an idol.

Evidently the people decided that because Moses was gone, they needed something to worship. But they shouldn't have been worshipping Moses because Moses was merely God's representative. His absence should not have affected their worship of God. Nonetheless, Aaron, who should have known better, gave in to their demands and created an idol. The Israelites resorted to idolatry because they did not have a solid understanding of who God is. Despite that, God repeatedly revealed Himself to the Israelites. Yet they still traded Him in for a material image with no power and forgot His words:

> I am the LORD your God, who brought you out of the land of Egypt, out of the house of slavery; you shall have no other gods before me. You shall not make for yourself an idol, whether in the form of anything that is in heaven above, or that is on the earth beneath, or that is in the water under the earth. You shall not bow down to them or worship them... (Exodus 20:2-5 NRSV).

In our society, we suffer from the same amnesia as the Israelites. We lose our understanding about who God is, and we trade Him in for material or symbolic idols and give them authority that belongs only to God. We forget that there are no substitutes for Him.

Remember that an idol is anything that you rely on, other than God, to make decisions. It is a person, place, or idea that controls your thoughts and actions. To destroy our reverence for God, the culture encourages us to idolize ourselves, our possessions, our loved ones, our political party, our race, our desires, our opinions, and more. Once we allow idols to usurp God's role in our lives, we will eventually abandon His standards too.

ACCEPTING WHO GOD SAYS YOU ARE

Keeping our reverence for God also means accepting God's view of our identity. Part of our human identity is divine because we are made in the image of the Creator (Genesis 1:27). We are also flawed and in need of God's salvation (Romans 3:23). God desires that we have a relationship with Him and that we allow Him to define us, despite how we feel. Ultimately, each one of us is a reflection of Christ. Your mistakes don't define you. Your actions don't define you. Your external circumstances don't define you. Your feelings don't define you.

And the way we view ourselves will determine the course of our lives. This is why it behooves us as Christians to regularly remind ourselves of who God says we are because the world will constantly bombard us with information that contradicts the truth of our identity.

This concept of self-absorption is certainly not new. It was apparent in the Garden of Eden and introduced to Adam and Eve by Satan, "You will be like God." Being like God means we are not subject to Him or anyone else. And while this concept is ancient, our American culture has begun to push it into the mainstream and advocate for it to be the basis of our laws and policy. It is the foundational principle of the new culture.[5] This is a dangerous trend, and ultimately, it will lead to the destruction of freedom. We are being trained to hold the flesh in high esteem and to do so in the name of compassion.

The biggest point of confusion about who we are in our society today is with regard to our role in marriage and sexual relationships. Because the culture has adopted a hedonistic perspective, it has also contorted God's view of who we are as men and women. God's chosen identity for us is now viewed as outdated, limiting, or discriminatory. But we cannot escape our identity in God. It is true whether we want it to be true or not.

Genesis 1 provides the fundamental blueprint for God's chosen identity for people. First, God makes mankind in His own image. In other words, He made us to be a reflection of Him:

> God said, "Let Us make man in Our image, according to Our likeness; and let them rule over the fish of the sea and over the birds of the sky and over the cattle and over all the earth, and over every creeping thing that creeps on the earth." God created man in His own image, in the image of God He created him; male and female He created them (Genesis 1:26-27 NASB 1995).

God then designed people to be in two categories: male and female. His intent was to make the two complementary to each other physically, spiritually, and emotionally. He designed them to create a family together by giving them the ability to procreate, or to "be fruitful and multiply" (Genesis:1:28).

The New Testament describes marriage as a reflection of the dynamic between Christ and the church. The Bible equates the husband's role with his wife to the role of Christ with His church. The husband must love his wife unto the point of his own death and sanctify her continually. A wife must respect and submit to her husband as he submits to Christ (Ephesians 5:22-32). While some read this and assume that it means that women are somehow inferior to men in the Bible's eyes, the opposite is true. The wife is the most valuable thing to her husband just as the church is the most valuable thing to Christ. The roles between husband and wife complement their intended identities in the kingdom of God. In other words, God's purpose for the roles of husbands and wives is not about value; it is about function. What this demonstrates is that not only are we supposed to be a metaphoric expression of God individually, but our relationships are to be also.

It is important to realize that God is not necessarily after a particular type of sexuality. He desires that we live in righteousness, because that is the only way He can truly commune with us. God cannot be intimate with us when we live outside of His standards. And being intimate with God is the only way we experience true freedom in this life.

But the culture tells us that nothing matters more than our desires, our convenience, and our happiness. In the world's view, you are the master of your own universe. Let's examine how American culture has gradually programmed us to idolize self-satisfaction, and further, how we have been convinced that giving in to our every desire is freedom.

INDULGING IS THE NEW FREEDOM

American laws should permit you to live freely, within established limits that promote and preserve constitutional principles, which, as we discussed earlier, are generally based on Christian ideals. One of the reasons that we are so quick to dismiss God is that we assume that we know better. We assume that our intentions, opinions, and desires are inherently good. The Bible makes it clear this presumption isn't true.

In 1873, Anthony Comstock created what became enacted as Comstock Laws, making it illegal to send "obscene, lewd, or lascivious," "immoral," or "indecent" material through the mail. It was a misdemeanor to sell, give, or possess obscene books, pictures, or the like. The world portrays Comstock as an "anti-vice activist." A *Teen Vogue* article called him an evangelical Christian who was influenced by a biblical story of Adam and Eve that influenced him to protect white, upper-class women's innocence. The article ridiculed him for his belief that women should be submissive to men and remain in the home. But Comstock also served in the Civil War for the Union army, fighting against the slave trade. Comstock eventually rose to political power and became the special agent to the US Post Office, allowing him to enforce the interception of pornographic material.[6]

In direct defiance of the federal Comstock Act, Margaret Sanger, avowed eugenist and racist, announced in the very first issue of the *Woman Rebel* that she would "advocate the prevention of conception" and that she would "impart such knowledge in the columns of this paper." It was at this time that Sanger and her group coined the term *birth control*.[7] In 1914, Sanger was charged with violating the Comstock Act for her distribution of her pamphlet called *Family Limitations*.[8]

Later, in 1921, Sanger founded the American Birth Control League, which led the effort for birth control with the intention of controlling "undesirable" populations and encouraging sexual liberation in women. The American Birth Control League is the earliest version of Planned Parenthood.[9]

In the 1950s, many conservatives sought to control the declining sexual standards in society. Despite these efforts, Hugh Hefner launched the first issue of *Playboy* magazine in 1953, featuring Marilyn Monroe on the cover. Hefner stated, "Publishing a sophisticated men's magazine seemed to me the best possible way of fulfilling a dream I'd been nurturing ever since I was a teenager: to get laid a lot."[10]

During the sexual revolution, liberals promoted openness and what they called progress, and they wanted to revoke laws that advocated a specific view of sexual morality. Theorists of the sexual revolution viewed any sexual repression, divine or traditional rules, or parental authority as barriers to personal happiness. The point was to affirm sexual gratification as the ultimate achievement; orgasm above all else because it would contribute to overall personal satisfaction. The movement also viewed femininity and modesty in a derogatory manner, at least as far as it disfavored or inhibited sexual independence.[11]

The culture of sexual liberation achieved a number of legal victories that helped propel the path forward.[12] The US Supreme Court afforded constitutional protection through a series of cases on obscenity, privacy, and sexual autonomy.[13] This includes *Roth v. United States*, in which the Supreme Court made it difficult to regulate obscenity and pornography.[14]

In 1960, Envoid became the first birth control pill available.

For the first time, this made it possible for a woman to control contraception without consulting with her boyfriend or husband.[15] And in 1965, in *Griswold v. Connecticut*, the Supreme Court ruled unconstitutional a Connecticut law that banned the use of contraceptives. Ruling for Planned Parenthood, the court created an implicit right to the constitutional right to privacy, a right that would later be used in cases like *Roe v. Wade* and *Obergefell*. *Griswold* prohibited states from banning contraceptives nationwide, ultimately becoming the first of many cases prohibiting a state from maintaining a moral prescription of sex.

No-fault divorce laws accompanied this revolution.[16] In 1969, California enacted the first no-fault divorce law under its governor, Ronald Reagan. In time, no-fault divorce became the law in all 50 states—the last state to pass it was New York in 2012.[17] The same year that California enacted the no-fault divorce law, Andy Warhol directed and released the first erotic film in America, *Blue Movie*. This birthed what has since become the Golden Age of Porn. Celebrities promoted pornography regularly.

To justify this shift, liberals advocated for the freedom of expression and equated it with the freedom of speech, even though they are not the same thing. Free speech is designed to protect the free exchange of ideas, like debates during an election. Freedom of expression protects nude dancing and pornography.[18] Freedom of speech serves the republic, while freedom of expression serves the flesh.

It didn't take long for the culture to adopt the idea that true freedom meant indulging in sexual appetites. In the mid-1950s and early 1960s, William B. Lockhart and Robert C. McClure, professors of law at the University of Minnesota, provided many of the arguments about how shaping and limiting sexual appetites undermined a free society.[19] These ideals naturally require adoption of relativism and denial of any moral absolutes. Justice William O. Douglas, writing in dissent in *Ginzburg v. United States* (1966), stated:

> Some like Chopin, some like "rock and roll." Some are "normal," some are masochistic, some deviant in other respects…But why is freedom of press and expression denied them? When the Court speaks of "social value" does it mean a "value" to a majority?[20]

Under this view, when we decide to limit free expression, we are appealing to a particular moral majority, and all those who do not heed to those beliefs are dismissed as the immoral, oppressed minority.

Biologist and professor Alfred Kinsey and his colleagues taught that sex was purely physical, akin to an animal appetite. He argued that sex was not a moral issue.[21] Kinsey contended that sex was a "normal biologic function" that was "acceptable in whatever form it is manifested."[22] Kinsey, whose research relied on pedophilic encounters, was a central inspiration for what is currently being taught to children in public school sexual education.

In 1973, the US Supreme Court created a new standard in *Miller v. California*, which ultimately led to the conclusion that most pornographic material was not obscene. This fueled the rapid growth of the pornographic industry. Also in 1973, in *Roe v. Wade*, the US Supreme Court again invoked the right of privacy to grant a national right to an abortion, banning states from prohibiting abortion before the first trimester of pregnancy.

The Supreme Court's decisions granted legal imprimatur to the moral decline of society. Chief Justice Warren Burger, writing in *Paris Adult Theatre v. Slaton*, which allowed for the regulation of adult movies in theaters, articulated the growing problem well:

> The sum of experience, including that of the past two decades, affords an ample basis for legislatures to conclude that a sensitive key relationship of human existence, central to family life, community welfare, and the development of human personality, can be debased and distorted by crass commercial exploitation of sex.[23]

By 1980, pornography was available on television through pay-per-view. And by the time the internet launched in 1993, pornography was widely available. With this increase in pornography came a slow acceptance of sexual acts that were once considered unacceptable, including same-sex intercourse. By the time *Playboy* created a website in 1994, a bipartisan Congress enacted the Defense of Marriage Act. The Act was intended to protect the right of states to recognize marriage as taking place only between a man and a woman.

Two years later, porn became so widely available that even children were viewing it regularly. The Communications Decency Act was signed in 1996 and was, in part, designed to prohibit individuals from transmitting or displaying obscene or indecent messages or material to people under 18.

From 1998 to 2009, the porn industry grew from $750 million to $4.9 billion dollars. One of the few restrictions on porn sites came in 2015, when Brock Turner was convicted of two counts of rape. The case was heavily covered by the media and the porn site xHamster instituted the "Brock Turner Rule," which prohibited videos of rape or other forceable sexual acts. This case is also famous because of the unbelievably light sentence Turner received for one of his crimes: six months in jail.

Ultimately, America's deregulation, acceptance, and wide promotion of pornography led to a broader sexual revolution that unraveled society's respect for marriage. It saw the biblical and once culturally acceptable view that sex was best confined to marriage to be restrictive and a violation of personal liberty.[24] This gradual acceleration of pornography was the impetus to society's acceptance of all sorts of sexual perversion and confusion today.

In 2003, in *Lawrence v. Texas*, the US Supreme Court held unconstitutional a Texas law criminalizing consensual sex between men—specifically, sodomy. Less than a decade later, the Supreme Court would go on to use the same substantive due process right of privacy used to uphold the right to contraception and abortion to also declare that states could no longer ban same-sex marriages. In 2011, when *Obergefell v. Hodges* was decided, the bipartisan federal law known as the Defense of Marriage Act allowed states to ban same-sex marriages and, at that point, as many as 35 states still did. *Obergefell* became a government prohibition on states that wanted to uphold a moral perspective of marriage.

After this monumental legal shift, a radical form of sexual progression made its way to Capitol Hill. In 2012, *Newsweek* called President Barack Obama the "First Gay President" because of his forceful support of gay rights, specifically because he instructed the attorney general of the United States not to defend the Defense of

Marriage Act during *Obergefell*.[25] And the Democratic National Convention officially promoted and supported same-sex marriages and dropped the word *God* from its platform.[26]

At this point, the term *liberal* no longer aptly described the proponents of this radical view of sexuality. The New Left was a Frankenstein version of the liberal, combining the views that Americans should have the right to explore all manners of self-expression and that those desires are one and the same with one's identity, meaning criticizing their behavior meant criticizing them personally.

In Lawrence Friedman's words, this new regime promoted "the republic of choice," in which the right "to be oneself" is of the utmost importance, and in which free expression is valued over self-control.[27] The New Left currently insists that the advancement of natural law ideals is an affront to the sexual preferences of all individuals and ultimately akin to racial supremacy. It is now said that the most disdainful forms of opposition in our culture are declaring moral sexual absolutes and stating biblical views of who men and women are.

The issue with changing the definition of marriage or the normal expectation for sex is that to do so results in no standard at all. Once you say marriage is not exclusively a union between one man and one woman, then the question is, What doesn't constitute marriage? Why can't it be three people or between an adult and a child or two children? The latter points about children are even more problematic given the trend toward sexualizing children and allowing them to make adult, life-altering decisions.

With this exaggeration of self-expression, the transgender movement easily ushered in a new reality in which biology is no longer respected. The slippery slope of affirming the sexual desires of everyone has led to the denouncement of fundamental truths about the differences between the sexes.

This rabid obsession with desire will infect the innocence of children. This is the last bridge of morality that the sexual revolution must cross in order to completely destroy the sexual moral compass of society. Children are a reminder that some level of sexual obscenity is inappropriate under some circumstances. But if sex is purely physical and morally neutral, what is the problem with sharing it with children?

We have found our way to a sinister place, where adults are openly and publicly advocating to teach kids about sex and show them pornographic material. Children are being encouraged to think about their sexuality as early as kindergarten and, even more disturbingly, the culture is beginning to relabel pedophiles as "minor attracted persons," referring to their deviancy as a sexual preference. This dangerous trend is approaching the point of no return for our culture. This will lead to the public promotion of children having sex with adults. It can be no other way.

This is why the government should not regulate to appease the emotions of the people. If this current trend succeeds, it will lead to the complete erosion of constitutional rights and an ideological caste system, meaning those who do not change their beliefs will be penalized and oppressed. Ultimately, such a society will destroy the laws that protect people whose beliefs do not conform to popular culture, especially Christians. This trend has already begun. The government is increasingly punishing religious people, schools, businesses, and organizations that will not submit to the new cultural norms.

KEEPING REVERENCE IN THE CHURCH

Recently, Florida Representative Greg Steube read from a Bible commentary about what the Bible says on the subject of gender identity. Afterward, Representative Jerry Nadler stated, "Mr. Steube, what any religious tradition ascribes as God's will is no concern of this Congress."[28]

But we cannot divorce our Christian heritage from our nation's successful advancement of liberty. One of the reasons our country is the most successful free republic in history is because we acknowledge some level of morality within our policies and laws. Getting rid of that moral foundation will ultimately destroy our nation's freedom.

Because of this and the fact that we are God's ambassadors, the church must uphold reverence for God and His standards and continue promoting the truth about who He says we are. At present, many churches have fallen prey to the culture's deceit to adopt unbiblical doctrines in the name of false compassion.

For one thing, God's mandates about sexuality are designed for our benefit and are a perfect fit for how He made us. Accepting the idea that men and women belong together spiritually, emotionally, and physically serves as acknowledgment that we accept who God says we are (Matthew 19:5-6).

While many consider these standards bigotry, God's standards for sexuality apply equally to everyone. They are not merely indictments against the gay or transgender community. His desire for us is sexual purity and morality. We *all* must make a decision to honor His standards no matter what our sexual desires. You may be heterosexual and married yet desire sex with someone who isn't your spouse. You may be single and want to have sex even though you do not have a spouse. The idea is that while we acknowledge these feelings, we do not give in to them. This includes refraining from sexual acts that God says are detrimental to our relationship with Him and detrimental for us emotionally and spiritually.

God is jealous for us (Exodus 34:14), and following idols means we are choosing to follow man's creation (Isaiah 2:8; Deuteronomy 27:15; Psalm 115:4; 135:15; Jeremiah 51:17; Jonah 2:8). Idolatry begins in the heart with longing and desire. When it, like all sin, is fully grown, it leads to death (James 1:15). That is, spiritual death. We begin to want something more than we want God and give it our allegiance. We worship ourselves and our desires, and they become our god. Matthew 6:24 states it this way: "No one can serve two masters; for either he will hate the one and love the other, or he will be devoted to one and despise the other. You cannot serve God and wealth." Likewise, you cannot serve both God and your desires. And you cannot serve both the truth and a lie (Romans 1:25 NASB).

The key to keeping reverence for God in a hostile culture is to remember who God is and remember who He says you are. I once heard that the best judges are those that care about being neutral arbiters of the law, not about being liked. I believe this is also the mark of a good church and a necessary character trait in every Christian. We should be concerned about representing God's truth accurately, not being liked by the world.

CHAPTER 5

HONOR THE GOLDEN RULE, PART 1

I n Luke, an expert in the law asked Jesus what he should do to inherit eternal life. Jesus replied, "Love the Lord your God with all your heart and with all your soul and with all your strength and with all your mind" and, "Love your neighbor as yourself" (Luke 10:27). To this, the expert asked Jesus how he could identify his neighbor.

To answer the expert's question, Jesus told the parable of the good Samaritan. In it, a man was attacked, robbed, and left for dead on the side of the road. A priest and a Levite saw the man, but both passed him by and continued their journey without helping him. Then a Samaritan saw the man, had compassion on him, and tended to his wounds. He also took him to an inn and left money for the innkeeper to take care of the man. Jesus asked the expert to identify who in the story had been a neighbor to the wounded man. Of course, he correctly identified the Samaritan. Jesus then told the expert to go and do likewise (Luke 10:25-37).

In addition to protecting your perception of God and your perception of yourself, to keep your conscience in our culture, you must also maintain a proper perception of others. That is, you must commit to doing to others what you would have them do to you (Matthew 7:12). This is widely known as honoring the golden rule.

The foundation for the golden rule is the belief that we are all made in the image of God, meaning we are all a reflection of Him. To honor the imago Dei (a Latin phrase that translates to "image of God"), we must see everyone we encounter as precious and valuable to God because He created them. Thus, we are to view everyone as innately valuable and worthy of dignity and respect.

But the culture tells us that nothing matters more than our desires, our convenience, and our happiness. That's why so many people are self-absorbed. When you are the central point of your life, God cannot be, and neither will your ability to respect others as God-created beings. This lack of respect is the basis for supremacy.

The most stubborn stain on American history is the oppression of black people in America. However, the fundamental, biblical principles of the Constitution bled through this racist stain, and eventually resulted in the nullification of the provisions that did not live up to the original intent of the Constitution and the Declaration of Independence. Some people cloaked their supremacy in Christianity, and that lie caused the public to implicate the church in America's greatest sin. This public shame often overshadows the double-edged truth that the Bible does not support racism and the Constitution helped eradicate invidious government discrimination. When Americans embrace the corrective power of the Constitution and its importance in keeping us from future atrocities, they will fiercely protect it. The Constitution recognizes the biblical truth that all men will seek to control one another if they receive too much power. Only God is supreme. Our constitutional rights are inalienable. That is, they are granted to us by God, and they must not be stripped away by any man.

AMERICA'S ORIGINAL SIN

Many of the Americans who drafted the Constitution agreed that slavery was a violation of the foundation of liberty and justice proclaimed in the Declaration of Independence. But they also removed Thomas Jefferson's explicit denouncement of the slave trade from the final version of the document, thus setting up a major conflict that would ensue during the drafting of the Constitution.[1]

During the drafting of the Constitution, the Northern and Southern delegates at the Constitutional Convention had to decide how to handle the issue of slavery. There was no question that the Southern delegates would never agree to abolish slavery in the Constitution, and they regularly threatened to abandon the Convention if the issue was on the table. But their hypocrisy was evident in the fact they did not want to be penalized for the slave population by direct taxation, yet they wanted to benefit from the slaves for determining representation in the House of Representatives.[2] The Northern states, wanting to punish the Southern states for the slave trade, advocated to make representation based only on the population of the free citizens of a state. Eventually, the framers agreed to a compromise that representation for the House would be determined by the free citizens of a state's population plus three-fifths of the enslaved people.

Representatives and direct Taxes shall be apportioned among the several States which may be included within this Union, according to their respective Numbers, which shall be determined by adding to the whole Number of free Persons, including those bound to Service for a term of years, and excluding Indians not taxed, three-fifths of all other Persons.[3]

Fredrick Douglass defended the clause this way: "The Three-Fifths Clause does not protect slavery. It recognizes that slavery existed at the time, but it did not guarantee it. In fact, it rewarded states that abolished slavery by giving them more representation in Congress."[4]

In addition to allowing the Southern states to keep the slave trade, the delegates also agreed to the Fugitive Slave Clause,[5] which allowed escaped slaves to be recaptured and included a provision prohibiting the abolishment of slavery until 1808. The Slave Trade Clause,[6] which was ultimately a moratorium on the slave trade, was an indication that the framers knew that slavery was a violation of the Constitution's foundational principles, and that is the reason the Southern states demanded this provision in the first place. Individual states were still free to prohibit slavery, but none did, until 1777, when Vermont became the first colony to ban slavery.[7]

Other than delegates from Southern states like Georgia and the Carolinas, few of the delegates defended the slave trade. Many of them, especially the Christians, were vehemently against the institution, like John Jay, Alexander Hamilton, and John Adams. But many ask why some of these delegates made public statements against slavery yet still owned slaves. Some reasons include that slaves were mortgaged like property to creditors, some could not run plantations without slaves, and more practically, blacks in some states would not be able to secure jobs under the oppressive governments.[8] Patrick Henry acknowledged that slavery was anti-Christian but said he felt that society placed him in a moral dilemma in which the only Christian response was to keep his slaves and treat them well. James Madison declared that "the whole Bible is against slavery" but he owned more than 100 slaves. Thomas Jefferson regularly opposed slavery but did not free his own slaves until his death.[9]

Nevertheless, the early American framers contributed to the hypocrisy of the establishment. While the Declaration of Independence stated that all men are created equal, neither the Articles of Confederation nor the early version of the Constitution explicitly outlawed slavery. Early congressional legislation distinguished between "citizens of the United States" and "persons of color," allowing the law to grant some rights to one group and not to the other.[10]

Ultimately, slavery was possible because too many people in general society accepted the erroneous belief that black people were subhuman, and therefore, they were inferior to whites. And the laws used this belief to justify discrimination against blacks.

LEGALIZING DEHUMANIZATION

Dredful Discrimination

Dred Scott was a slave owned by James Emerson of Missouri. Scott eventually moved to the free territories of Illinois, then Wisconsin. Afterward, Scott and his wife, Harriet, moved back to Missouri. Emerson died, and Scott attempted to purchase his freedom from Emerson's widow, but she refused the sale. Scott and Harriet sued for their freedom in a Missouri state court in St. Louis, where Scott's abolitionist lawyers argued that Scott's residence in free territories had freed them both under Missouri's long-standing doctrine "once free, always free."

In 1850, the Missouri court held that Scott was free, but shortly afterward, the Missouri Supreme Court reversed that decision. After this, Emerson's widow left the state, and Emerson's brother, John Sanford (incorrectly spelled Sandford on the court documents), held control of Emerson's estate, and it is his name that appears on the Supreme Court case. Because Sanford, as a resident of New York, was not subject to suit in the state of Missouri, Scott's lawyers filed in a federal district court, which also declared Scott free.

Eventually, in 1857, the case went to the US Supreme Court. In the 7-2 decision, Justice Taney wrote that while blacks could be citizens of a particular state, they could not be national citizens, and thus, could not sue in federal court. Consequently, Scott's case should have been dismissed. This was unstable reasoning, though, because under the Privileges and Immunities clause, the Constitution requires that if one state considered Scott a citizen, all states and the federal government had to also. And, even if that wasn't the case, Article III allows federal courts to handle cases between citizens of different states.[11]

Taney went further and determined that Scott had, in fact, never been free, and that the Missouri Compromise's "once free, always free" doctrine was unlawful because Congress did not have the power to abolish slavery. This also unraveled the ability of states to enter the Union as free states. This demolished the independence of the states and their ability to acknowledge free blacks.

Despite the explicit language in the Declaration of Independence and the preamble of the Constitution, Taney rejected that blacks were entitled to the liberty promised by the new government.[12]

The dissents from justices John McLean and Benjamin R. Curtis were highly critical. Further, the Northern states were furious at the opinion. Republican Senator Charles Sumner of Massachusetts predicted that "the name of Taney is to be hooted down the page of history."[13]

Eventually, Dred Scott and his wife gained their freedom when they were bought by the Blow family, who freed them in 1857. Harriett lived to see the Civil War and the enactment of the Thirteenth Amendment in 1865.[14]

Dred Scott is also noteworthy because it created unenumerated rights, which is the judicial philosophy that the Constitution promises rights that are not explicitly written in the document. This doctrine continues to haunt American justice and is evident in cases like *Roe v. Wade* and *Obergefell v. Hodges*. Uunenumerated rights were also used in cases involving parental rights,[15] and in the right of criminal defendants to be found guilty beyond a reasonable doubt.[16] The goal of unenumerated rights is to recognize rights that are clearly established in our history and tradition and are implicit in the Constitution's promises.

Now, it is obvious that *Dred Scott* would not have been possible if the framers had made slavery explicitly unconstitutional by declaring that people could not be property. While the framers never said that the Constitution banned slavery, the foundational principles of the document implicitly declared that it does.[17] Other than the declarations of liberty for all, other provisions prove this conclusion.

The Constitution does not guarantee slavery at the federal level, and it allows Congress to limit or abolish the institution. Provisions like due process are clearly inconsistent with slavery.[18] Slavery is an example of a bill of attainder, and the Constitution explicitly prohibits them.[19] The Constitution also prohibits the seizure of persons without legitimate lawful authority.[20]

As mentioned earlier, the Privileges and Immunities Clause is devastating to slavery because it guarantees that Americans cannot be deprived of their rights when they travel between states.[21] At the time of *Dred Scott*, black people could be citizens in some states, and then travel to a Southern state and be denied their liberty.[22]

Legal precedent is also generally against the interpretation in *Dred Scott* and any pro-slavery reading of the Constitution because the courts are required to interpret the Constitution as pro-freedom whenever possible.[23] And under the clear statement rule, the Constitution is interpreted in favor of liberty unless Congress enacts a law stating otherwise.[24]

From Civil War to Civil Rights

In 1863, during the Civil War, President Abraham Lincoln signed the Emancipation Proclamation. It freed only the slaves of the Confederate States and strategically deprived the South of its gravy train created by free slave labor. Most say that this was the ultimate strategy of the Emancipation Proclamation, though there is ample evidence that Lincoln thought slavery was immoral. Still, a presidential executive order was a questionable way of proclaiming the end of slavery.

In 1865, Congress passed the Thirteenth Amendment, which formally abolished slavery in America. Lincoln was assassinated by John Wilkes Booth before the constitutionally required rat-ification of the Thirteenth Amendment by three-fourths of the states took place. In this case, 27 of the 36 states agreed with the amendment.[25]

> Neither slavery nor involuntary servitude, except as a punishment for crime whereof the party shall have been duly convicted, shall exist within the United States, or any place subject to their jurisdiction.

This was followed by the passage of the Fourteenth and Fifteenth amendments and the Reconstruction Act of 1867, which required all states to provide equal protection to blacks. As a result, Recon-struction contributed to more than 90 percent of black men being registered to vote. In reaction to Reconstruction, many whites per-sisted in upholding the supremacy they enjoyed by creating paths around the new constitutional amendments. For example, even though black men were legally allowed to vote (women could not vote until 1920), many states created measures to ensure they were not eligible, such as tests that were designed for them to fail. That is, tests that white men did not have to take in order to vote. One such measure was the grandfather clause, which stated that a man could vote only if his ancestor voted before 1867. This was clearly a problem because most blacks were enslaved at that time. By 1940, only three percent of black men could vote in the South.[26]

Separate, but Equal

Once the Reconstruction era ended in 1877, Southern states enacted black codes, laws that were designed to enforce segregation against blacks. These are often called Jim Crow laws, named after a minstrel routine that was a derogatory parody of black people.[27] Early attempts to stop segregation were thwarted by the courts. For example, the earliest Civil Rights Act of 1875 was declared unconstitutional by the Supreme Court in the Civil Rights Cases of 1883.

In 1896, in *Plessy v. Ferguson*, the Supreme Court reviewed Louisiana's Separate Car Act of 1890, which required separate seating for whites and blacks on all transit. The court implied that separate treatment was not necessarily unequal. It stated that the Constitution extended only to political and civil rights, such as voting and jury service. But the court concluded that the law did not guarantee blacks "social rights," such as where they could sit in a railway car. The majority said that "if one race be inferior to the other socially, the constitution of the United States cannot put them upon the same plane."[28] Moreover, the Thirteenth Amendment was only about slavery, not segregation. Ultimately, the court ruled that "separate, but equal" in accommodations, including schools, was constitutional. In a famous lone dissent, Justice John Marshall Harlan asserted that the Constitution was "color-blind" and that all American citizens should have equal access to civil rights.

After the *Plessy* decision, segregation grew throughout America, not just in the South. Segregation made it difficult for blacks to travel, stay in hotels, eat in public, enjoy entertainment venues, receive a proper education, and much more. For nearly 100 years, from the time after the Civil War until 1968, blacks were forced to endure oppressive treatment. Blacks who resisted the laws were arrested, fined, harassed, or killed.[29]

One of the other elements we will explore later when we discuss justice is the fact that many former Confederate soldiers, some

who were also members of the Ku Klux Klan, became police officers, judges, and politicians. This put them in positions of authority that allowed them to impose their supremacist views on blacks.
This also allowed prisons, which were essentially labor camps, to
be used to convert blacks in prisons to redesigned slaves.

Many white supremacists persisted in rising in power. In 1867,
Ohio resident Allen Granbery Thurman ran for governor on a platform that primarily promoted banning blacks from voting. He
lost, but then won a seat as a US senator and spent his time in
Congress blocking measures designed to support equal rights for
blacks.[30] The terrors of this era are well documented, so for our
purposes, we'll leave most of the details out of this discussion and
focus on the legal landscape.

In 1954, the Supreme Court unanimously dethroned the separate but equal doctrine in *Brown v. Board of Education*. In it, the
court held that segregating public schools based on race denied
black children equal protection of the laws under the Fourteenth
Amendment. Some criticize this opinion not for the holding, but
because the reasoning relied on social science statistics that said
segregation produced a sense of inferiority that detrimentally
impacted black children. This was true, the court reasoned, even
if the physical environment and resources of the school were equal
to those in white schools.[31]

We should pause to look at this too. The social science statistics merely provided supplemental proof for something that we
all know. Segregation between blacks and whites must always be
looked upon suspiciously because of America's history. We cannot
tolerate even the slightest indication of racial supremacy between
these groups.

Ending Persistent, Severe, and Pervasive Discrimination

Initially proposed by President John F. Kennedy, the Civil Rights Act of 1964 was signed by President Lyndon B. Johnson. The comprehensive federal law was designed to ban discrimination based on race, color, religion, or national origin. Title I of the Act guarantees equal voting rights and removes onerous registration requirements biased against minorities. Title II prohibits places of public accommodation involved in interstate commerce from discriminating against protected classes. Title VII, which added sex to the protected classes, bans discrimination by schools, employers, or trade unions involved in interstate commerce or doing business with the federal government. The Civil Rights Act also bans segregation in public schools and assures equal treatment in the distribution of funds in federal programs.[32] This Act was followed by other protective measures, such as the Voting Rights Act of 1965 and the Fair Housing Act of 1968, which aimed to end discrimination in connection with renting and selling homes.

The Civil Rights Act was put on the fast track through Congress and was heavily criticized and opposed by Southern Democrats. The employment sector was particularly combative because many interpreted the provisions as a government mandate on who private businesses could hire, fire, and promote.

By this time, America had reached the point that the government was the only mechanism that could correct the supremacist hole our culture had fallen into. Despite the constitutional amendments, many whites refused to give up the supremacy the law had afforded them for so long. To justify the continued bigotry toward blacks, many claimed that protecting blacks through federal legislation amounted to preferential treatment and would reduce legal rights for whites. Others felt that America was long overdue for this change and that people could not be trusted to treat blacks fairly unless the law forced them to.

The debates on the Civil Rights Act were continuous and contentious throughout the legislative process. In a nationally televised debate on the bill on March 18, 1964, Senator Hubert Humphrey (D-MN) said, "Our fellow Americans, who happen to be negro" have been denied the right to vote and equal access to public accommodations, and he called the mistreatment of blacks a "moral issue." Senator Strom Thurmond (D-SC) said that the bill bestowed "preferential rights on a favored few." He said the bill would abandon "a government of laws in favor of a government of men." He claimed the bill had the governmental power to decide what was discrimination and accused the government of giving in to civil disobedience, no doubt referring to the large-scale demonstrations and protests of civil rights activists at the time. He claimed that the bill would take away constitutional rights from others.[33]

But the measure had strong bipartisan support. And a large cohort of religious groups supported the Civil Rights Act. More than 6,000 Christian, Catholic, and Jewish representatives attended a National Interreligious Convocation at Georgetown University to discuss the bill with senators who were undecided. In April, before the vote, Protestant, Catholic, and Jewish students held a prayer vigil at the Lincoln Memorial. Students took turns praying 24 hours a day throughout the legislative process and during the Senate debates until passage of the bill.[34] On June 19, the bill, with some edits, passed the Senate by a vote of 73–27.[35]

White supremacists responded to the civil rights laws with

protests and increased backlash against blacks. The Civil Rights Act of 1964 was immediately challenged in *Heart of Atlanta Motel v. United States*.[36] Heart of Atlanta Motel refused to allow blacks to book rooms even after the passage of the Civil Rights Act. The motel argued that Congress had exceeded its power and could not regulate who the motel did business with. The court ruled unanimously that Congress could regulate hotels because they rented rooms to out-of-state guests, and such practices could be regulated under the Commerce Clause.

THE PERVERSION OF CIVIL RIGHTS

As we reviewed in the last chapter, many in America have allowed their desires to usurp God's view of identity: His and ours. This has produced an open door for the idolatry to distort what it means to treat people with respect and dignity.

At the time the Civil Rights Act was enacted, Congress recognized that blacks were subjected to discrimination that was persistent, severe, and pervasive, and that such treatment required congressional intervention. Congress has always been hesitant about adding more protected classes to civil rights legislation. The law is reserved to protect us from discrimination based on immutable aspects of our identity.

But once the culture began to embrace sexuality as akin to identity, a movement was unleashed to use civil rights laws designed to help blacks and women and turn them into laws that provided protection for sexual inclinations.

In 2011, when the Supreme Court declared in *Obergefell* that no state could ban same-sex marriages, the government opened the door to a perversion of civil rights. After this decision, a trend began to force those who were morally opposed to such unions to participate in them.

Many, including Christians, have demonized people for refusing to participate in same-sex marriage ceremonies, often equating the dissenters with white supremacists. But let's examine why these religious defectors are not like racial segregationists.

In *Masterpiece Cakeshop*, Colorado sued a bakery because it refused to create a custom cake for gay unions. The facts, which are often buried by the media, are as follows: Owner Jack Phillips sold many baked goods to the same-sex couple prior to the suit. By all accounts, he knew the gay couple for years and had a good relationship with them. When the couple decided to get married, they asked Phillips to create a custom cake. While Phillips was happy to accommodate the couple by providing generic products in the business, he could not, in good conscience, create a custom cake for their ceremony because he does not believe gay marriages are moral. Colorado officials compared his beliefs to the beliefs of a segregationist and ridiculed him for his biblical positions.[37]

Ultimately, the Supreme Court looked at these facts and decided that the Constitution required the state to treat his beliefs neutrally and the officials' statements proved that they were biased against Phillips. The Supreme Court held that hostility to religion is a violation of the Free Exercise Clause and ruled for Jack Phillips and his business, Masterpiece Cakeshop.

Recognize that what is going on here is the creation of a different kind of caste system—one where the government will not protect you unless you adopt new beliefs about sexuality. Let's look at a very interesting case about a 100-year-old Catholic adoption agency, *Fulton v. Philadelphia*.

In this case, a Philadelphia Catholic adoption agency had been serving the city for a century. Being Catholic, it always had requirements that the couples that it certified for adoption were married men and women. The city eventually created an ordinance that required the agency to agree that it would certify same-sex couples, even though the agency was never approached by any such couples. This was likely because there were dozens of other agencies in the city for couples to choose from. Regardless, the city said that if the agency wanted to continue operating its adoption ministry, it had to agree to certify same-sex couples if it was asked. The Supreme Court ruled against Philadelphia.

Now do Jack Phillips or the Catholic adoption agency operate their businesses the ways they do because they think heterosexual people are above gay people? Are they attempting to protect an established caste system between people with different sexual preferences? No. But the comparison can easily turn sincere religious adherents into cultural outcasts.

In 1983, in *Bob Jones University v. United States*, the Supreme Court held that nonprofit private universities that engage in racially discriminatory admissions on the basis of religious beliefs do not qualify as tax-exempt organizations under Section 501(c)(3) of the US Internal Revenue Code.[38] Generally, all public and private educational institutions are exempt from taxation because they provide qualitatively valuable public services. The court stated that the university did not serve a legitimate public purpose because of its racial supremacist practices.

Sometimes this case is used to argue that nonprofits that hold biblical views of marriage should also lose their tax exemption status. However, this argument is incorrect for the social reasons I mentioned above. Racial discrimination should always be examined strictly in light of America's history.

But people rarely discuss that the law acknowledges that sex discrimination is different than racial discrimination. The courts and even the Civil Rights Act explicitly allow sex discrimination because there are real differences between the sexes. There are obvious and practical reasons why the government might treat men differently than women, like in the case of public accommodations such as bathrooms and locker rooms. But America's government is beginning to treat this type of separation as unlawful. America is exchanging laws based on objective, scientific principles in favor of those that protect shifting, subjective emotions.

The impetus to this legal crusade against biological sex standards was ushered in with the help of a justice who is considered conservative. In *Bostock v. Clayton County*, the Supreme Court held that federal employment discrimination law's ban on discrimination "on the basis of sex" includes discrimination based on sexual orientation and gender identity.[39] Justice Neil Gorsuch, who wrote for the majority, acknowledged that when the civil rights law was written, the term *sex* meant biological sex. But Gorsuch and the others still decided that it was actionable under Title VII when, for example, a funeral home fired a man who decided to "live and work full-time as a woman."

The decision effectively added protected classes to the Civil Rights Act, meaning that the court's decision usurped the power of Congress.

In *Bostock*, the court views the Constitution as an evolving document that we should interpret based on popular opinions. But our rights don't rely on popular opinions. Our rights are inherent—like biology. Today's society is abandoning the foundational principles of truth to justify ideological supremacy. This decision abandoned the simple truth about the unquestionable differences between men and women and adopted the lie that sex is based on subjective beliefs.

The court's decision resulted in a cascade of actions by both federal and state governments to enforce this dangerous standard of discrimination in other contexts, like grade-school bathrooms.

CIVIL RIGHTS VERSUS SOCIAL SUPREMACY

In today's culture, Christians must understand how to accurately evaluate the issue of civil rights. To be sure, the Bible speaks to the issue of racism. The Bible outlaws slavery in Exodus 21:16 ("He who kidnaps a man, whether he sells him or he is found in his possession, shall surely be put to death" NASB 1995). In another example, Peter refused to eat with Gentiles because he feared he would offend other Jews, but Paul corrected Peter (Galatians 2:11-14). And, as we reviewed earlier, the Bible is clear about God's desires regarding our sexual identity.

Mainstream media, politicians, and others often compare anyone who believes in a biblical sexual ethic to white supremacists. If Christians are unable to evaluate issues involving race and sexuality biblically, they will be deceived into thinking like the world. They will be manipulated into believing that compassion requires the acceptance, affirmation, and even approval of morals that depart from God's standards. This is a lie. Nothing trumps God's standards. The Bible denounces slavery and racial supremacy, and it also defines sexual morality. Christians cannot lose sight of these truths.

If Christians are unable to evaluate issues involving race and sexuality biblically, they will be deceived into thinking like the world.

But as Christians, we cannot consider ourselves better than nonbelievers. This is not about worth. Rather, it's about spiritual standing. Our desires can be just as toxic as those of non-Christians, but our mistakes are covered by Christ's blood. Being Christian means even more, however. It provides a divine motivation to live in a way that is purpose-driven and inspiring. When you live like this, you realize that life is about more than what we want. Sometimes we get our desires by following the divine path. Sometimes we don't. Nonetheless, we follow the path. This is because being a Christian is a glorious ride through life. Yes, there is an eternal reward for becoming a disciple of Jesus Christ, but the earthly reward isn't a bad deal either.

CHAPTER 6

HONOR THE GOLDEN RULE, PART 2

T he ultimate way to uphold the golden rule is to honor someone's right to life. This right is inseparable from the acceptance of the imago Dei and our inherent connection to our Creator. There is no more fundamental right in a free society than the right to life. Once a society legitimizes the unjust killing of another human being, the moral compass of that society will be crippled until that injustice is corrected.

What we've learned from the extermination of lives in America, Nazi Germany, Rwanda, and other countries is the powerful effect supremacy has on a society. The exaltation of the self produces a rabid indifference to life and unleashes the most grotesque aspects of human nature. Perhaps nothing reveals this truth more than the detestable practice of abortion.

SUPREMACY AND REPRODUCTION

In 1883, Francis Galton, a British statistician and half cousin of Charles Darwin, coined the term *eugenics*.[1] Social Darwinism is the root of eugenics, and as we've discussed, it promotes belief in the concept of "the survival of the fittest." Ultimately, eugenicists believe that humans can mimic nature's ability to rule out the unfit by taking proactive measures to prevent reproduction in people deemed to be genetically undesirable.

Planned Parenthood's founder, Margaret Sanger, was a well-known, self-proclaimed eugenicist who coined the term *birth control*. In 1915, she was arrested in New York for mailing diaphragms. To avoid facing trial, she fled to Europe, where she was influenced by sexologist Havelock Ellis. Sanger adopted his beliefs about sterilization of the poor, and Sanger herself believed that parents should have to be approved by the government to have a child.[2] Sanger said,

> Every single case of inherited defect, every malformed child, every congenitally tainted human being brought into this world is of infinite importance to that poor individual; but it is of scarcely less importance to the rest of us and to all of our children who must pay in one way or another for these biological and racial mistakes.[3]

Sanger referred to the poor as "human waste" and proclaimed that they and other human "weeds" must be exterminated.[4] Sanger's *The Birth Control Review* was well known for Nazi propaganda and articles by Nazi officials. She organized the first World Population Conference in Geneva, Switzerland, in 1927.[5] Sanger was connected to other white supremacists, including Lothrop Stoddard, who wrote *The Rising Tide of Color Against White World Supremacy*, in which he argued,

> If white civilization goes down, the white race is
> irretrievably ruined. It will be swamped by the triumphant
> colored races, who will eliminate the white man by
> elimination or absorption…We now know that men
> are not and never will be equal.[6]

Back in the States in 1916, Sanger and her sister, Ethel Byrne, opened an illegal birth control clinic in Brooklyn, New York. The clinic was in a neighborhood of immigrants, including Italians and Jews. Sanger worked to enforce her supremacist beliefs using contraception on these populations. Sanger and her sister were arrested and spent a month in jail.[7]

Meanwhile, by the 1920s, intellectuals, professionals, and others adopted eugenics and made it a "full-fledged intellectual craze" in America.[8] Theodore Roosevelt reportedly supported the eugenic research of the Cold Spring Harbor laboratories.[9] Many proponents of eugenics held prominent positions at Ivy League schools like Harvard and Yale, and the theory was taught at 376 universities and colleges.[10] Harvard was "more central to American eugenics than any other university"—its staff and alumni heavily promoted eugenics by writing articles, publishing textbooks, and lobbying governments to enact eugenics laws.[11]

The prejudices of Sanger and others in the early twentieth century advanced the laws and policies that eventually led to the legalization of forced sterilization. As governor of New Jersey in 1911, Woodrow Wilson signed a law mandating forced sterilization of "the feeble-minded." And in 1927, Supreme Court Justice Oliver Wendell Holmes wrote an opinion in *Buck v. Bell*, holding that forced sterilization statutes were constitutional.[12] He wrote for the majority:

We have seen more than once that the public welfare
may call upon the best citizens for their lives. It would
be strange if it could not call upon those who already
sap the strength of the State for these lesser sacrifices,
often not felt to be such by those concerned, in order
to prevent our being swamped with incompetence.
It is better for all the world, if instead of waiting to
execute degenerate offspring for crime, or to let them
starve for their imbecility, society can prevent those
who are manifestly unfit from continuing their kind.
The principle that sustains compulsory vaccination
is broad enough to cover cutting the Fallopian tubes.
Three generations of imbeciles are enough.[13]

The Supreme Court's decision fueled the eugenics movement
with "legitimacy and considerable momentum."[14] By 1931, 28 states
had legalized eugenic sterilization.[15] Between 1907 and 1983, Carrie Buck, the "feeble minded white woman" who was the plaintiff
in *Buck*, was one of more than 60,000 people involuntarily ster-
ilized in the nation.[16]

In 1921, Sanger founded the American Birth Control League.
But to distance itself from eugenics and its influence in Nazi Germany, the organization changed its name to Planned Parenthood
in 1942.[17] It is recognized that Sanger was not directly referring to
abortion when she discussed the role of eugenics in birth control.
But, as US Supreme Court Justice Clarence Thomas put it, "Sanger's
arguments about the eugenic value of birth control in securing 'the
elimination of the unfit'[18] apply with even greater force to abortion, making it significantly more effective as a tool of eugenics."[19]

LEGALLY ALIVE: THE
LEGALIZATION OF INFANTICIDE

In 1973, in *Roe v. Wade*, the Supreme Court, for the first time, held that abortion was a constitutional right. The justices said that whether it be founded in the Fourteenth Amendment's concept of personal liberty and restrictions upon state action, or in the Ninth Amendment's reservation of rights to the people, both are broad enough to encompass a woman's decision to terminate her pregnancy.[20] The court's inability to determine where in the Constitution this right was derived would eventually lead to *Roe's* demise in 2022.

Most notably, the court declared that unborn babies are not people under the Fourteenth Amendment, and they are not entitled to the right to life.[21] This is the moment the law permitted the dehumanization of the unborn, and we still have not recovered from this grave error. The court further noted:

> Texas urges that, apart from the Fourteenth Amendment, life begins at conception and is present throughout pregnancy, and that, therefore, the State has a compelling interest in protecting that life from and after conception. We need not resolve the difficult question of when life begins. When those trained in the respective disciplines of medicine, philosophy, and theology are unable to arrive at any consensus, the judiciary, at this point in the development of man's knowledge, is not in a position to speculate as to the answer.[22]

But the court recognized that the State may have an important interest in safeguarding health, maintaining medical standards, and "protecting potential life."[23] The court admitted that there was at least some point in a woman's pregnancy that the state's interest in protecting unborn babies would supersede this mysterious privacy right, which means that the privacy right was not absolute.[24] But the court never reconciled the obvious issue between its conclusion that states have an interest in protecting unborn babies and the conclusion that unborn babies are not alive for purposes of the Constitution. Here, we find a wide schism in the law.

Ultimately, the court created a confusing trimester framework that would determine when a state could or could not prohibit abortions. *Planned Parenthood v. Casey* would alter this framework by holding that a state could not place an undue burden on a woman's ability to seek an abortion before the first 24 weeks, which was determined to be the point of viability (when the baby could possible survive outside of the womb).[25]

As happened with slavery and forced sterilization, the law legally dehumanized unborn children and provided legal justification for their destruction at will. But the Constitution does not, would not, and should not grant a right to illegitimately kill another human being. Such a freedom should never exist in any free society. The unborn are people who are entitled to the right to life, and that enumerated right should be applied to everyone without question.

Sanger's views and her purpose for the establishment of Planned Parenthood are often shielded from the organization's efforts. In her autobiography, she proudly recounts her address to the women of the Ku Klux Klan.[26] And in a 1939 letter to Clarence Gamble, she explained the organization's outreach to the black community:

The most successful educational approach to the Negro is
through a religious appeal. We don't want the word to get
out that we want to exterminate the Negro population,
and the minister is the man who can straighten out that
idea if it ever occurs to any of their more rebellious
members.[27]

Despite Planned Parenthood's persistent attempts to distance itself
from the sordid history of its founder, Margaret Sanger, it cannot erase the facts, which clearly demonstrate how closely aligned
abortion and supremacy truly are.

According to a 2015 study, nearly 80 percent of Planned Parenthood's surgical abortion facilities were located within or near
minority neighborhoods. The Guttmacher Institute revealed that
in 2014, even though black women only accounted for 13 percent
of the US population, they had upward of 28 percent of abortions.
And by now, we've all heard the devastating statistic that in New
York City (not far from the site of Sanger's first clinic), more black
babies are aborted than born.[28] Sanger's own words reveal her heart:

Birth control itself, often denounced as a violation of
natural law, is nothing more or less than the facilitation
of the process of weeding out the unfit, of preventing
the birth of defectives or of those who will become
defectives.[29]

Many people argue that although Planned Parenthood is rooted in
this shameful past, the organization has a positive impact on society and does not subscribe to Sanger's views. But a bad tree cannot

bear good fruit. And Planned Parenthood's continued targeting of low-income individuals and minorities for abortions should convince you that it is fundamentally rooted in evil ends.

Without being fooled by the deceptive advertising that tells you that abortion is akin to freedom or women's rights, notice that the organization employs the same disgusting, dehumanizing rhetoric as the Nazis and white supremacists. While it is unequivocal that a fertilized egg is in fact alive for all biological purposes, the organization promotes the lie that unborn children are "clumps of cells," "masses," and compares them to tumors.[30]

In 2022, Democratic politician Stacey Abrams said, "There is no such thing as a heartbeat at six weeks. It is a manufactured sound designed to convince people that men have a right to take control of a woman's body away from her."[31] These are inconceivable lies that are as destructive as the idea that black people are three-fifths of a person. Such dehumanization gives us the justification we need to dismember and kill the unborn and get rid of them because they are an inconvenience to us.

In many of my conversations with people about abortion, including self-proclaimed Christians, many argue that abortion is sometimes necessary. They argue that birth defects or even the possibility that the child will end up in poverty, in an abusive home life, or in foster care justifies abortion. In their eyes, we should spare the child from what we perceive to be a difficult upbringing.

But we must remember that we do not have the right to decide whether someone else's life will be worth living. Whether they have a disability or unfortunately end up in an abusive home life, people can rise above the most adverse circumstances to be a force for good. Their stories should be authored by God, and human beings have no authority to decide that a child is better off dead than alive.

Like any form of illegitimate exercise of power, the expectations become more brazen. Unsurprisingly, many now suggest that women should be allowed to abort their babies because of the race, sex, or disabilities of the child.

In 2019, the Supreme Court upheld an Indiana law requiring that facilities dispose of aborted fetuses in the same way as human remains. But the court declined to decide on the second provision of the law, which prohibited abortion providers from performing abortions if they know "that the mother is seeking the abortion solely because of the child's race, sex, diagnosis of Down syndrome, disability, or related characteristics."[32] In his concurrence, Justice Thomas emphasized "that abortion is an act rife with the potential for eugenic manipulation."[33]

Over the past decade, Iceland and Denmark aborted nearly all unborn children prenatally diagnosed with Down syndrome. The United States aborts approximately 67 percent of those babies.[34] In 2021, only one Democrat supported a measure banning abortions of children with Down syndrome.[35] In Asia, the culture's preference for male children led to a striking population imbalance between males and females.[36] When abortion was first presented, it was advertised as rare and safe. Now, politicians openly advocate for abortion up until birth.[37]

In 2022, in *Dobbs*, the Supreme Court shockingly overruled *Roe* and *Casey* and held that the Constitution, including the Equal Protection Clause, did not infer a right to an abortion, meaning that states could prohibit abortion at any point during a pregnancy.[38] This was a partial correction of abortion case law, but *Dobbs* did not correct the legal supposition that unborn babies are not human beings that are entitled to the right to life under the Fourteenth Amendment.[39]

The development of abortion law resembles that of slavery laws, specifically the Three-Fifths Compromise. Remember that the central issue was whether slaves should be counted as persons for the purpose of state representation in the US House. The opposers argued that slaves should not be counted because slaves were property in slave states, not persons. The slave states denied that slaves were merely property, but rather, said they were considered persons in some respects, like in criminal law. [40]

Slavery and abortion both seek to dehumanize the targeted group. If the Constitution defends anything, it must defend life. When our laws begin to parse out personhood, we should be immediately skeptical. Consider this apt expression of this analogy:

> To be sure, in some jurisdictions, slaves were at once regarded as persons and as non-persons, in the criminal law and in property, respectively. These jurisdictions recognized the reality of the natural personality of slaves for some purposes, for example, to subject them to criminal liability, but they endorsed the fiction that slaves are merely property for others. The legal status of the unborn was the reverse. In some jurisdictions, the unborn were regarded as persons in property but not in the criminal law. These jurisdictions recognized the reality of the natural personality and humanity of the unborn for some purposes, and they endorsed the fiction that they do not exist as such for others.[41]

The authors of this scholarly piece express that these considerations should highlight the alarming way that *Roe* treats the legal status of the unborn. The court said that "unborn children have been recognized as acquiring rights or interests by way of inheritance or other devolution of property, and have been represented by guardians ad litem." But the court still concluded that "the unborn have never been recognized in the law as persons in the whole sense" because the interests involved "have generally been contingent upon live birth." The irony here is that slaves were also not "recognized in the law as persons in the whole sense."[42]

Fetal personhood is not widely accepted, even among conservatives. To be sure, Justice Brett Kavanaugh declared in his concurrence in *Dobbs* that the "Constitution neither outlaws abortion nor legalizes abortion."[43] That said, fetal personhood should be the next frontier in the pro-life movement. Fetal personhood would entitle the unborn to equal protection of the laws under the Fourteenth Amendment, which would include homicide laws. Such a declaration from the US Supreme Court would outlaw abortion in America.

JESUS CHRIST IS SUPREME

There are plenty of scriptures that reflect the truth that every unborn child is a creation of God. Psalm 139:13-16 (esv) is my favorite:

> You formed my inward parts;
> you knitted me together in my mother's womb.
> I praise you, for I am fearfully and wonderfully made.

Wonderful are your works;
my soul knows it very well.
My frame was not hidden from you,
when I was being made in secret,
intricately woven in the depths of the earth.
Your eyes saw my unformed substance;
in your book were written, every one of them,
the days that were formed for me,
when as yet there was none of them.

The golden rule means that our interests are not supreme to someone else's well-being. We must demonstrate compassion and truth as the correct expression of love for another person. Christians must repeatedly defend God's standards for how we treat others. And we must dismantle the arguments that using or killing someone is appropriate to pursue a person's own ends. In the same way that the church has been guilty of defending racial supremacy, it has joined forces with the culture to defend abortion.

Ultimately, Jesus Christ is supreme above all others.

The Son is the image of the invisible God, the firstborn
over all creation. For in him all things were created:
things in heaven and on earth, visible and invisible,
whether thrones or powers or rulers or authorities; all
things have been created through him and for him. He
is before all things, and in him all things hold together.
And he is the head of the body, the church; he is the
beginning and the firstborn from among the dead, so
that in everything he might have the supremacy. For

God was pleased to have all his fullness dwell in him, and through him to reconcile to himself all things, whether things on earth or things in heaven, by making peace through his blood, shed on the cross (Colossians 1:14-20).

We must begin by acknowledging the proper hierarchy. God is first. We are below and beneath Him, and all our desires, emotions, and confidences must be submitted to Him. We know that the culture will never fully adopt a biblical point of view, but as Christians, we must keep our consciences so that we can always advocate for God's perspective on every issue. We cannot let ourselves become a mouthpiece for the kingdom of darkness by embracing society's lies about who God is, who we are, and how we treat one another. Keep your conscience at all costs.

We know that the culture will never fully adopt a biblical point of view, but as Christians, we must keep our consciences so that we can always advocate for God's perspective on every issue.

CHAPTER 7

LIVE WITH PURPOSE

J oseph was one of Israel's 12 sons, and because he was born to Israel at an older age, Joseph was favored by his father (Genesis 37:3). After Israel gifted Joseph with a multicolored robe, Joseph's brothers knew that their father loved Joseph the most, and they were envious and resentful of him (verse 4).

Joseph shared with his brothers dreams he had that indicated he would one day reign over them (verses 5-11). That was the last straw for Joseph's already-envious brothers. They kidnapped Joseph and sold him into slavery (verses 27-28). Eventually, Joseph ended up in Egypt and, because the Lord was with him, he became the trusted servant of Potiphar, the captain of the guard for Pharaoh (Genesis 39:1-4).

But drama ensued when Potiphar's wife repeatedly tried to seduce Joseph because he was handsome and well built (verses 6-10). Despite his repeated refusals, Potiphar's wife eventually trapped Joseph in a room with her when no one was home and told him to sleep with her. She grabbed his coat and pulled him toward her (verses 11-12). Joseph fled, leaving behind his coat (verse 13). Rejected, Potiphar's wife lied and told the servants and her husband that Joseph raped her, using his coat as her evidence (verses 13-18). Potiphar put Joseph in prison, where he remained for years (verses 19-20).

Despite this wrongful imprisonment, the Bible says the Lord was still with Joseph. While he was in prison, he was offered another leadership position as keeper of the prison (verses 21-23). Several years into his prison sentence, Joseph met two employees of Pharaoh, who were thrown into prison for offenses committed against him. They had dreams, and Joseph interpreted their dreams for them. Joseph predicted that one, a cupbearer, would be out of prison in a few days. Joseph asked the cupbearer not to forget him when he was free. The cupbearer does get out of prison, but he forgot about Joseph (Genesis 40:9-15, 21, 23). Two more years went by (Genesis 41:1).

Then Pharaoh had two dreams that caused him to become restless because he could not figure out what they meant. No one else could either, as Pharaoh asked all the usual suspects for advice. When the magicians and wise men failed to interpret the dreams, the cupbearer finally remembered Joseph, and recommended that Pharaoh consult him (verses 1-12).

After a shave and a shower, Joseph came before Pharaoh, and, giving all credit to God, he interpreted Pharaoh's dreams (verses 25-36). Declaring that Joseph has the "Spirit of God," Pharaoh hired Joseph as his right-hand person, and Joseph became the second-most-powerful man in Egypt (verses 37-45).

Eventually, Joseph was reunited with his family, and he saved them from famine (Genesis 42–45). His forgiveness of his brothers is notable because he attributed all the wrongs done against him to God's ultimate purpose of bringing Joseph to his position of stature and power (Genesis 45:4-8).

Joseph's story is a compelling illustration of how purposeful our lives become when we are walking with God. God was able to use seemingly unfortunate events to benefit Joseph and to further His ultimate plan. Because Joseph was faithful, God used Joseph to influence government at the highest level, even though the government's leaders were not believers in the one true God.

As Joseph's life demonstrates, your dedication to God and a heart inclined to serve others will inevitably lead you to your divinely inspired purpose. And you will be less susceptible to deception and manipulation from the world around you because you will be focused on God. As you grow in your relationship with God, He will refine your character and use you to impact others according to His agenda (Romans 8:29).

THE KINGDOM AGENDA

When a court makes a decision, that decision applies only to that court's jurisdiction or its territory. For example, when a state supreme court decides a case, that holding is binding only in that state. When the US Supreme Court decides a case, that holding is enforceable throughout the country.

Contrarily, God's jurisdiction is unlimited. He is king over all creation, and like any king, He has a kingdom.[1] Jesus said, "My kingdom is not of this world" (John 18:36). What He meant is that although He is king over this world, His kingdom extends beyond the physical. His kingdom originates in heaven, which means it derives from a spiritual source.[2]

Because of this, God's agenda focuses on the spiritual and the eternal, not just earthly concerns. God's plan for every believer is that they commit to fulfilling His will in, with, and through their lives while on earth. Dr. Tony Evans calls this principle the kingdom agenda, and he defines it as the visible demonstration of the comprehensive rule of God over every area of life.[3]

Living according to the kingdom agenda will permeate all aspects of your life. It is not just what you do when you are in church. It is not just about going to church. It is who you are, what you believe, how you behave, and the choices you make. Remember that the moment you were saved through Jesus Christ, His Spirit was implanted within you (2 Corinthians 1:22). Because of this, God's kingdom is not just an external purpose you are trying to discover. God's kingdom is also within you (Luke 17:21).[4]

> *Living according to the kingdom agenda will permeate all aspects of your life. It is not just what you do when you are in church. It is not just about going to church. It is who you are, what you believe, how you behave, and the choices you make.*

As a branch can bear fruit only when it is connected to a tree, so can we bear the fruit of God's kingdom only when we are connected to Him (John 15:4). When you walk with Christ, God's kingdom will spring out of you like fruit from a tree.

Abiding with Christ means you are abiding with the Word of God (John 1:1). God's Word is truth (Psalm 119:160). Jesus is the

Word made into flesh, which means that He is the personification of truth (John 1:14; 1 John 5:6). When you abide with Christ,
you are choosing to abide in truth. Truth is the absolute standard
by which reality is measured; it is God's viewpoint.[5] This means
that, as a Christian, you must be consistently walking with God
and abiding in His Word in order to produce fruit.

Now, even though you are a Christian and you have access
to truth, it's possible for you to choose to live without it. That is,
rather than live according to God's kingdom agenda, you end up
living according to His adversary's agenda. That adversary is Satan.
Understand that there are only two realms in creation: God's kingdom and Satan's kingdom.[6] While we are all born into Satan's kingdom, everyone who trusts Jesus Christ as their Savior is transferred
from Satan's kingdom to God's kingdom (Colossians 1:13). The
foundation for God's kingdom is truth, but the foundation for
Satan's kingdom is deception.[7] Satan is the quintessential tyrant,
perpetually rebelling against God's authority and seeking to establish his own kingdom with his own agenda.

First Timothy 4:1 warns that Christians can depart from the faith
and instead, heed "deceiving spirits and doctrines of demons" (NKJV).
This should show you that Christians can choose to live according to
Satan's deception and further his agenda instead of God's. Those who
are not Christians are already furthering Satan's agenda. We are all
under the rule of one realm or the other, whether we know it or not.

LIFE, LIBERTY, AND THE PURSUIT OF HAPPINESS

The Declaration of Independence says that our unalienable rights
entitle us to "life, liberty, and the pursuit of happiness." This

naturally brings us to question whose view of life, liberty, or the pursuit of happiness should prevail. Let's examine this.

John Locke (1632–1704) coined the phrase "pursuit of happiness" in *An Essay Concerning Human Understanding*. When Thomas Jefferson wrote the Declaration of Independence, he borrowed the phrase from Locke. Locke's concept of happiness did not equate happiness with pleasure, property, or the fulfillment of our desires. He distinguished what he called "imaginary" happiness from "true happiness."[8] Locke wrote:

> The necessity of pursuing happiness [is] the foundation of liberty. As therefore the highest perfection of intellectual nature lies in a careful and constant pursuit of true and solid happiness; so the care of ourselves, that we mistake not imaginary for real happiness, is the necessary foundation of our liberty.[9]

Locke differentiated pursuits that benefit our greater good from pursuits that merely satisfy our whims, which he classified as leading only to imaginary happiness. At the same time, Locke believed that the ideas of original sin or innate characteristics were merely mythological views.

While Locke made a keen observation about the separation between true happiness and imaginary happiness, he ignored the spiritual source of true happiness. He continued:

> If it be farther asked, what moves desire? I answer happiness and that alone. Happiness and Misery are the names of two extremes, the utmost bound where

we know not…But of some degrees of both, we have very lively impressions, made by several instances of Delight and Joy on the one side and Torment and Sorrow on the other; which, for shortness sake, I shall comprehend under the names of Pleasure and Pain, there being pleasure and pain of the Mind as well as the Body…Happiness then in its full extent is the utmost Pleasure we are capable of, and Misery the utmost pain.[10]

This is where Locke's insights fall short. Happiness does not always equate to pleasure. And pleasure certainly does not always equate to happiness. Sometimes we choose to make a decision that will lead to suffering, but we are still happy about it. For example, when you are led by God, happiness often doesn't move desire, obedience does. Obedience will often trump pleasure when your ultimate goal is to walk in God's will.

From a Christian perspective, misery is not always a good indication of whether we are living in God's abundant life. Consider Job, whom God offered to Satan to torment for the sake of testing Job's righteousness and his allegiance to God. Consider Jesus. Ultimately, when you say yes to following God, you accept that God is concerned with your development, not your happiness—at least, not your immediate happiness. Romans 5:3-5 says:

Not only so, but we also glory in our sufferings, because we know that suffering produces perseverance; perseverance, character; and character, hope. And hope does not put us to shame, because God's love has been poured out into our hearts through the Holy Spirit, who has been given to us.

When you consider the pursuit of happiness from a biblical standpoint, you realize that you must be after an eternal joy, not a temporary fix. This is why Paul calls us to "fix our eyes not on what is seen, but on what is unseen, since what is seen is temporary, but what is unseen is eternal" (2 Corinthians 4:18).

Locke did recognize that false pleasures promise immediate gratification but often cause pain. The abuse of alcohol, for example, provides short-term euphoria but produces unhealthy mental and physical effects. Still, Locke connected the "pursuit of happiness" and human liberty. He argued that happiness is the foundation of liberty, to the extent that it allows us to make decisions that will provide a promising future, instead of decisions that provide only immediate gratification.[11] Thus, we can choose to abstain from sexual acts that defile us, or decide to eat well rather than indulge in greasy foods and sweets. We do not have to be slaves to our desires and passions, like animals.[12] We have a choice, and we can choose to override the dictates of our carnal cravings.

But rather than consider Christianity the only truth, Locke treated it as the best choice among many views about the eternal future. If there is nothing after life, then our actions mean nothing. We can live for our desires only. But if death is just the beginning of a new life, then we should live with that truth in mind. Locke argued that hedonism may lead to everlasting suffering, while a life of righteousness only costs us to give up some carnal pleasures. In essence, Locke said, the Christian life is the best bet to make on our eternal future.[13]

With this in mind, choosing Jesus because you are afraid of what will happen to you in the afterlife is one of the shallowest reasons to choose Him. Many people embrace Christ for this reason, but once you realize what God is truly offering with salvation in Christ, you realize salvation from eternal death (meaning separation from God) is just one aspect of the deal. Because of this, a Christian has no reason to fear death. To die is to be at home with Christ and away from the body (2 Corinthians 5:8), away from the world we don't belong in anyway. Death is liberation for the Christian because we never truly die. Being free from the fear of death should distinguish us from the outlook of others in the world.

I bring all this up because it's important to understand how the government should balance protecting our pursuit of happiness with liberty. While Locke argued that Christianity and its path of virtue were the wisest choices, some argue that the government should not prescribe or mandate paths to happiness and leave that up to the individual.[14] The problem is that the government must have some limits on how people can pursue their own happiness because the government cannot create laws merely to serve people's carnal pleasures. Put another way, "laws must have boundaries because happiness for one person may be misery for another."[15]

Ultimately, the government must have a foundation on which to determine what liberty means in light of personal happiness. And it must decide that some rights are more important than some pursuits of happiness. America's founders chose to submit to a theocratic view of humanity, loosely based on Christianity, for guidance on how to structure the government. While this does not bind each American to a Christian philosophy, it does provide the government with a foundation to guide its decisions. Laws should protect the established God-given rights, and therefore, cannot exist to feed every carnal inclination.

Those who want to truly promote liberty in America are obligated to dedicate themselves to serving the country. They must actively pursue making a more perfect union to ensure the legacy of America as the freest and most successful nation in history. As President John F. Kennedy stated, "Ask not what your country can do for you but what you can do for your country."[16] Similarly, Christianity says that the greatest in the kingdom of heaven are those who serve God's purposes.

MOTIVATED BY PURPOSE

There are many people in America who claim to be Christians. But there are few laborers for Christ (Luke 10:2). As believers, it's vital that we live out God's kingdom agenda. This means making sure we're not lukewarm followers of Christ who claim His name but don't want to proclaim His Word. Many professing Christians are unwilling to stand up to the culture because they do not want to bear the cost of criticism, cancellation, or controversy. But that is what we signed up for.

The call to follow Christ is a call to be in conflict with the culture, or the world. Jesus warned us that joining His team means the world will hate us (Matthew 24:9). We often forget this in the midst of a culture where we rarely or only mildly suffer for our faith. In places like China and the Middle East, being a Christian takes on a whole new meaning because of the high cost involved.

No matter what the degree of separation between us and the culture, it will always exist, and we must stand firm even when the confrontation becomes intense. Christians throughout history have faced this reality to varying degrees. But despite the risk, we must press forward and persist in proclaiming God's truth and advancing His kingdom.

The question that comes next is how we find our purpose within the context of our lives, which includes where we live, the cultural atmosphere, the legal landscape, our families, and our lifestyles. First, we must examine our sphere of influence. Consider the opportunities you have each day to be a witness for Christ, both in word and action. This may range from exemplifying Christ as a stay-at-home mom raising children, bearing witness to Him as a senator in the US Congress, or a combination of both. Maybe you are a mom with a career, and you are influencing both your family and an audience outside your home. Whatever your position, your calling is still the same. You are to be a visible manifestation of Jesus Christ in your everyday life with whomever you encounter, whether family, friend, or foe.

We all have a role to play in God's kingdom agenda, and you should spend time consulting God about what He wants you to do. Paul tells us in 1 Corinthians that one plants a seed, and another waters it. We must each contribute to the harvest in our assigned roles as God's co-laborers. And ultimately, God is the one who makes the seeds grow (1 Corinthians 3:6-9).

We may be tempted to think that our purpose in life is to be happy, wealthy, and esteemed. But our purpose is much deeper than that. Knowing God and making Him known are our highest callings. Though we may achieve happiness, financial independence, and public respect, they are only byproducts of our purpose—they are not the goal.

Knowing God and making Him known are our highest callings. Though we may achieve happiness, financial independence, and public respect, they are only byproducts of our purpose—they are not the goal.

A key aspect of finding purpose is fulfilling a need in the church or community. You must seek to provide a service to those around you. Because Christianity and many other religious traditions teach service as an expression of faith, many of the people who serve in our society are religious. For example, religious people are significantly more likely than those who are minimally religious or nonreligious to volunteer or donate to the poor within the last week.[17]

A November 2022 study published by the journal *Preventative Medicine* found that people who found their lives to be purposeful had about a 15 percent risk of premature death from any cause during an eight-year tracking period.[18] This was compared to a 37 percent risk of premature death for those with the lowest level of perceived purpose. The study included about 13,000 Americans over 50, and it found that the results were true across people of all races and ethnicities. The study defined purpose in life as the extent to which people perceived their lives as having a sense of direction and goals.[19]

These results, as well as the survey's general definition of purpose, demonstrate that people in general marginally understand that we all need a direction in life. What's missing from this definition is the extent to which that purpose is motivated by our desire to achieve God's will for His kingdom. And this can be manifest in various ways. There are many different avenues to explore, and this can include a path in government, as with Joseph.

RELIGIOUS SERVICE IN A SECULAR SOCIETY

As it turns out, the benefits of religiously motivated service are not just good for us personally or for those we serve. It has a staggering and positive influence on our national economy as well. In a unique survey conducted in September 2016, researchers found that religion contributes nearly 1.2 trillion dollars to the socio-economic value of the nation's economy. The study, published in the *Interdisciplinary Journal of Research on Religion*, found that religion's economic contribution qualifies as equivalent to the world's fifteenth largest national economy. The contribution would be more than the top tech companies, including Google, Apple, and Amazon. It's also more than America's top six oil and gas companies.[20]

Religious ministries offer services such as care of the homeless, drug and alcohol recovery programs, hospitals, schools, youth mentoring programs, scholarships, disaster relief, foster care, legal services, and much more. For example, Samaritan's Purse aids disaster relief efforts around the world. Joni and Friends assists those with disabilities.

The vast majority of religious nonprofits provide their services for free or at a reduced cost compared to providers in the same industries. In large part, this impact is why religious nonprofits are tax exempt. But despite the undeniably positive impact of faith-based service, many people demand that religious nonprofits lose their tax exemption status or worse, lose the ability to continue offering services to the public.[21] This is due primarily to the ideological collisions that have taken place between the religious and the culture over the past few decades.

After *Obergefell*, the government threatened many religious adoption service providers that would not agree to certify same-sex couples for adoption. Many religious providers in Massachusetts, California, and other states were forced to close for not compromising their convictions on this issue. As a result, the government-run adoption services were overwhelmed because they relied heavily on the services that the religious nonprofits provided to the community. Many of these agencies had operated for 100 years or more, even before the government began caring for orphans, and thus, the government has never had to sustain the full load of the foster needs.

In one case we discussed earlier, Philadelphia instituted an ordinance demanding that all the adoption agencies in the city must agree to certify same-sex couples, or they could not continue offering their services. The archdiocese and several foster parents affiliated with one Catholic organization sued the city, arguing that the requirement violated the Free Exercise and Free Speech Clauses of the First Amendment.

In a surprising unanimous decision from the US Supreme Court, all the justices said that Philadelphia could not force the 100-year-old religious adoption agency to abandon its convictions in order to continue contracting with the government to provide foster services. The ruling in *Fulton v. Philadelphia* was a welcome halt to the destruction of many religious providers trying to pursue their purposes in a hostile culture. Unfortunately, many of the providers in other cities were forced to close prior to this decision and have not since reopened. Despite the undeniable benefit of services provided by religious organizations in our country, the culture still attacks religious individuals and groups because their beliefs are in conflict with the world's.

RESISTING THE PRESSURE

We are at a crucial point in time when the American culture does not respect or value religion in our society. While the culture may acknowledge the benefits of the services that religious organizations offer, they do not believe that value outweighs the danger of our countercultural beliefs. Our ability to continue living out God's purposes will become increasingly difficult as secular ideology strays further away from biblical perspectives. As we pursue our purposes, we must be prepared to do so with a willingness to persevere in spite of the cultural pressure we will experience.

When a potter works with clay, he applies heat and pressure to make the clay more malleable so it can be molded. The heat and pressure we experience as Christians can be to our benefit or detriment. God can use heat and pressure from the culture, from personal hardships, or from other circumstances to mold us into His image. But the culture can likewise use heat and pressure to mold us into its desired image.

Christians are commanded not to conform to the world's image (Romans 12:2). Our goal, then, is to ensure that whatever pressure we experience is used to conform us to Christ's image.

Romans 12:2 also speaks of renewing our minds, which is a central element of overcoming pressure from the culture. We are often deceived because we believe the world's lies, and those lies shape our thinking and actions. Over time, we knowingly or unknowingly abandon our convictions because we absorb the world's perspectives, oftentimes on subjects we do not completely understand. The world will always take advantage of our ignorance, which is why a lack of knowledge can destroy God's people (Hosea 4:6). We have to decide that we will commit to being tools for God, and that we will educate ourselves on relevant issues so that we cannot be fooled out of our convictions.

James 4:4-5 warns us that we should not be friends with the world because such friendship creates a rift in our relationship with God. We cannot serve two masters, and neither the world nor God will share us with the other (Matthew 6:24; John 15:18; 1 John 2:15). Understand that both God and the world want your loyalty. Simultaneously, we are also fighting against our flesh, that tyrant inside of us that wants to rule and squelch the Holy Spirit. And the world knows how to appeal to the flesh.

Remember that the world, and consequently the culture, belongs to Satan. God's original intention was for the world to belong to man. He gave man dominion over the earth in the Garden of Eden, but Satan deceived Adam and Eve and convinced them to disobey God, which successfully transferred their authority over the earth to Satan. As it stands, Satan still rules the world. Thus, when we talk about the influence of the world, we are really talking about the influence of Satan.

While God wants you to love Him, love others, and fulfill His purpose for your life, all for the furtherance of His kingdom agenda, Satan's goal is to influence you in the opposite direction. He wants to entice you to love yourself and the world more than God so that your actions lead you to a life devoid of divine purpose. When Satan controls your motivations and your life, you are furthering his agenda.

Keeping your conscience requires several daily commitments. Every day you must commit to loving Christ, commit to loving others, and commit to fulfilling God's purpose for your life. This powerful trifecta will help you to stay busy fulfilling God's kingdom agenda.

DIVINE PURPOSE IS ADDICTIVE

To experience God working in your life is an exhilarating feeling. The unfavorable consequences that can result from being a Christian do not compare with the joy of knowing Jesus Christ. You live every day knowing you are part of a larger plan, and that propels you toward your next act of obedience. Overall, my testimony as a follower of Christ is designed to inform, inspire, challenge, and edify you. I am a witness that God can do anything with your life when you're willing to be a vessel for Him. The purposeful Christian life is challenging and fulfilling.

In the next section, I'll dive into the enlightening and transformative information I've learned on this divine path. My experiences have immersed me in three key fields: justice, education, and media. These fields encompass key aspects of our society and our views on these broad issues will impact our personal and political choices in many areas of our lives.

These are also subjects that Christians can often become deceived about. I want to convince you to become knowledgeable in these fields. If you can get involved, whether as an employee, a volunteer, or an advocate, please do. But ultimately, you should have at least a general understanding of how justice, education, and media work so you can be an informed, influential Christian.

Justice is thoroughly covered in the Bible, and the biblical principles relating to this field also happen to have shaped many aspects of the American justice system. We'll explore the good, the bad, and the ugly. And we'll look at the racial conflicts that often pervade this topic and produce heated division within the church.

Education also happens to be one of my biggest passions. Despite the fact I am a constitutional lawyer and the matter of justice permeates my life, I started my walk with God by working in education, and teaching changed me in a way that I won't ever forget. I found that education can make or break a student, and for that reason, it is the area that I believe is most in need of Christian laborers. Without a proper education consisting of moral, academic, and civic instruction, today's young people will be very easy to deceive and control as they become adults.

Of the three fields, media has a truly significant influence on the public, and I believe it's also the most hostile to Christianity. It has the power to influence almost all other industries, including justice and education. This is the area in which I believe Christians are having the least impact. We should find our way into areas of news, entertainment, and social media to strategically spread God's truth to the world. We should also find and support those who publicly speak truth and defend their ability to do so.

PART 3

AREAS OF INFLUENCE

CHAPTER 8

ESTABLISH JUSTICE

The statue of Lady Justice symbolizes America's goal to balance freedom and protection. She wears a blindfold and holds a perfectly balanced scale in one hand and a sword in the other. The blindfold advances impartiality. Justice presupposes the inherent worth of all people and administers the appropriate remedy while remaining neutral to the parties involved. Lady Justice holds the scales high, demanding balance between personal liberty and proportionate punishment. With her other hand, Justice holds a sword prepared to demolish behaviors and attacks on the safety of the republic's people.

The Bible's view of justice is similar but narrower. If the depiction of Lady Justice were to include biblical justice, the sword in Lady Justice's hand would represent the Word of God. In the Bible, justice is constantly linked with righteousness (Deuteronomy 32:4; Job 37:23; Psalms 33:5; 97:2; 99:4; Isaiah 28:17; 51:5; 56:1; 32:16; 33:5; Amos 5:24; Romans 3:26). To be righteous is to live in alignment with God's commandments, refraining from sin and quickly repenting when we fall. Righteousness requires an intimate relationship with God (John 14:15, 21) and not just acknowledgment of His Word. When we are committed to righteousness, we are in a better position to achieve justice because the two are inextricably linked (Deuteronomy 32:3-4; Proverbs 11:11; 14:34).[1]

For this reason, our laws must be in line with God's standards. We cannot develop unjust laws that either proscribe what God demands or permit what God forbids. At the same time, we must treat all people as divinely created beings (Proverbs 14:31) without affirming all that people desire. Justice enforces God's standards in an impartial way.

And when we create just laws, they must be applied justly. There are laws that are explicitly neutral but can be misapplied or disproportionately applied to certain groups or individuals. This is injustice too. This is why we must not only protect the text of the law, but we must also hold accountable those who apply the law.[2]

As Christians, our goal is first and foremost to proclaim Christ to all. One way we do this is by demonstrating His impartial love and justice in our advocacy of political and social concerns. When we choose to be an advocate of justice, we must remember that we represent God's kingdom, and our advocacy must align with His standards.

When we choose to be an advocate of justice, we must remember that we represent God's kingdom, and our advocacy must align with His standards.

AMERICAN JUSTICE

America's governmental structure is designed to prevent tyranny, which is the quintessential unjust government. One way to avoid tyranny is to ensure that we do not have a government that consists of one person who serves as judge, jury, and executioner. Thus, America divides governmental power as a means of protecting justice.

For example, America elects dozens of people to create our laws. Congress, or the federal legislative branch, creates the federal laws. We elect hundreds of individuals to fill two separate houses of Congress for this purpose. And every state has a legislative branch that is patterned after the federal version. This system ensures that many people decide what laws are passed. As Christians, we should always ensure that we vote for representatives who will pass laws that are in accordance with God's view of government and righteousness, and we should advocate for them to do so.

The executive branch of the state and federal governments enforce the laws. For example, the Department of Justice, the Federal Bureau of Investigation, the Drug Enforcement Agency, and several others are responsible for enforcing federal, civil, and criminal laws throughout the nation. In the state and local governments, the state appoints law enforcement personnel at all levels to handle the task. Law enforcement does not include only the police. Lawyers and others who prosecute the laws are also considered part of law enforcement. While this group of people enforces the laws, they do not have the authority to create them. They do, however, have the very crucial power to decide whether they will enforce the laws justly.

When the text or application of a law is questionable, the judicial branch will analyze those laws to ensure they comport with constitutional requirements. After both sides present their arguments, the courts can nullify, alter, or uphold the law or application of the law. For this reason, all judges and justices (judges who sit on the supreme courts of the state and the nation) should be neutral arbiters who are committed to moral and just decision-making. Moreover, judges should stay within the bounds of their positions by analyzing the law and avoid creating new laws with their decisions because lawmaking is a legislative function.

Judges are also given major authority in our justice process and are sometimes the sole arbiters for trials called bench trials. They are vital decision-makers in our criminal justice system because they often determine the prison sentences for those who are convicted of crimes. Because they have the authority to decide how much of someone's freedom to take away, judges should be carefully vetted and selected by the public for state and local benches; by the president, who appoints them to the federal benches; and by the Senate, who consents to such appointments.

Our culture has increasingly become aware of the importance of judges, specifically justices on the US Supreme Court. These are the most important positions in the judiciary because they are the final authorities on the application of the country's Constitution, which is the supreme law of the land.

CHRISTIANITY AND THE LAW

Crime is not necessarily sin, and sin is not necessarily a crime. The two frequently overlap, but they are not the same. In his law dictionary, William Blackstone defined crime as "a breach and violation of the public rights and duties due to the whole community, considered as a community, in its social aggregate capacity."[3] And sin is defined as a transgression of the divine law which is an offense against God.[4] In other words, when we commit a crime, we violate our duty to the community. And when we sin, we violate our duty to God.

While sin and crime are different, it's possible to commit one and not the other. Christians are usually bound to obey earthly laws, meaning that a violation of an earthly law may also constitute sin. See, for example, Romans 13:1, which says, "Let everyone be subject to the governing authorities, for there is no authority except that which God has established."[5]

God was the first to instruct mankind about right and wrong, righteousness and sin. He did so by issuing commandments or laws—divinely inspired laws that dictated human behaviors within the community of God. There is a parallel between the supreme law of the land and God as the divine legislator.[6]

As mentioned, God's original intent for us was to be subject only to Him, in that He would be our sole governor. Then when kings ruled over God's people, God expected those kings to be subject to Him and to serve as His representative before the people. Modern government is assigned the same task: to be God's representatives and execute and uphold His laws among the people.

Today, society often separates our laws from their divine origin, although some people still recognize the law's moral undertones. As with most other subjects in American culture, people have largely divorced themselves from religious entanglements. Some claim that the Age of Enlightenment's "signal achievement was to break the existing link between law and religion."[7]

But the two are inextricably linked. Divine law and earthly law are both tied to society's agreement about what is right and wrong, and that determination must be based on a standard outside of our desires, lest it change with our whims. The standard of right and wrong for our society must be based on God's commandments, which never change.

> *The standard of right and wrong for our society must be based on God's commandments, which never change.*

And whether we like or not, many of our criminal laws derive from the Bible. The following crimes that exist or have existed throughout history derive from biblical prohibitions, including homicide (Exodus 21:12; Leviticus 24:18; Numbers 35:16-19); assault/battery (Exodus 21:18, 22-25; Leviticus 24:19-20; Deuteronomy 27:24); sex crimes, including adultery, rape, seduction, and forbidden sexual partners (Exodus 22:16; Leviticus 18; 20; Deuteronomy 22:22, 25-27); theft, including kidnapping, burglary, and fraud (Exodus 21:16; 22:1-3, 8; 23:4; Leviticus 19:11, 35; Deuteronomy 24:7; 25:13-16); damage to property, including injury to slaves and animals (Exodus 21:20-21, 26-27, 33-34; 22:4-5, 13-14; Leviticus 24:18); falsehood and slander (Leviticus 5:20-26; 19:16; Numbers 5:31; Deuteronomy 19:18-19; 22:19; 27:25); witchcraft, blasphemy, and other misuses of God's name, apostasy, and idolatry (Exodus 22:17; Leviticus 19:26, 31; 24:10-23; 26:1; Deuteronomy 13:2-12, 13-19; 16:21; 17:1-5; 27:15); and rebellion against authority (Exodus 21:15, 17; 22:27; Leviticus 19:32; Deuteronomy 17:9-13; 21:18-21).[8]

Diving deeper, the biblical law as well as American criminal law require that the arbiters take into account many of the same elements when calculating the guilt or innocence of a defendant. Let's examine the quintessential crime of murder as an example. Let's begin by acknowledging that murder is a sin and a crime for the same reason. We accept as a community that other people have dignity and worth and their lives are valuable and none of us have the right to take someone else's life from them. From a biblical perspective, the imago Dei commands that we acknowledge that we are a divine creation that deserves honor and respect. This foundation presupposes that murder is wrong. But the inquiry does not stop there.

Both the divine law and American criminal law take into account an important element: intent.

In the Bible, Exodus 21:12-14 classifies murder in two ways. One, whether the killing was premeditated—namely, whether the killer was lying in wait or hunting his victim. And two, whether the murder was "an accident allowed by God."[9] The factors that the Bible uses to determine whether the murder was an accident are whether the killer previously hated the victim (Exodus 21: 4, 6, 11) or the killer committed the act unintentionally (Exodus 22:2-3). The Bible also orders different punishments for intentional killings and unintentional killings.[10]

Likewise, in American criminal law, there must be an *actus reus*, meaning an intentional act, and a *mens rea*, an intentional mind. The law recognizes the varying levels of culpability by assigning different degrees of murder. First-degree murder is premeditated, intentional murder and comes with the strictest punishment, often life in prison or death. Second-degree murder is intentional killing without premeditation. This often means the killer murdered his victim during

a "heat of passion." The law school's typical fact pattern when teaching prospective lawyers this iteration of murder involves a spouse
who walks in on his wife in the act of adultery and, in a rage, kills
his wife and or her lover. The killer's actions in this situation are not
excused, but the law recognizes the difference in intent by enforcing
a lesser punishment than that for premeditated murder.

Then there is manslaughter, which is usually an unintentional,
accidental killing from reckless behavior, like drunk driving. These
are general proscriptions; some states structure their statutes differently. For example, some states will assign first-degree murder
charges to an unintentional killing committed during an intentional
felony. Felonious assault leading to murder, even without intention-
ality, can often be prosecuted as a first-degree murder. This was the
method prosecutors used in their case against Derek Chauvin for
the killing of George Floyd. The prosecution alleged that Chauvin
criminally assaulted Floyd, and during the commission of that felonious assault, Floyd died. As a result, the prosecution charged him
with first-degree murder without having to prove intent.

And both criminal law and biblical law excuse killing for reasons of self-defense, defense of another, or during war.

As you can see, the judgments of divine law and secular law
are similar, especially as they relate to violent crime. The connec-
tions between the Bible and the criminal law cannot be ignored.
They span millennia.

When the divine foundation of our laws is separated from secular law, the culture's ability to administer justice within the system is jeopardized. That leaves us with a system that usurps God
and becomes a tyrant on the people, whether through oppressive
laws or the unjust application of just laws. Just as we have seen in

our examples of historical tyranny, when we remove God from the authoritative equation, we are bound to abuse our fellow man. The Bible makes clear that this is a dangerous situation for people (Exodus 20:3; Deuteronomy 5:7; 6:4-5).[11]

So while a justice system is a divinely inspired and necessary aspect of any society—one that is meant to protect the members of the community and uphold the moral principles for prosperity—it is susceptible to corruption from the people who serve in that system. People can and do rob the system of justice through intentional actions or ignorance.

Our job as Christians, and even more broadly as Americans, should be to closely scrutinize our justice system with the intent of improving it. Unfortunately, not everyone has the same perspectives about the problems and how they should be solved. And we shouldn't assume that a political party has the answer, even if they claim to. While some Christians find affinity in the Democratic party because of its perceived emphasis on criminal justice reform and race relations, that doesn't mean the party's policies fix those problems. Contrarily, if we examine the Republican party's embrace of conservative social issues, we will find that not all Republicans are conservatives or Christians. We cannot assume that a party will do what is right simply because they promise to. Christians on both sides of the aisle must hold their political party accountable. But, for us to do that, we must be informed.

CRIMINAL JUSTICE FLAWS

My mother was a crime documentary junkie. When I was young, she would braid my hair and we would watch all the great murder mysteries. To this day, I'm still a true crime fanatic. Many people ask me why I watch such shows. For some, true crime is too violent and real. But I am fascinated by how the law catches up with the most clever and prolific criminals. For me, true crime is an education in pursuing justice. I've developed a profound respect for our justice system, while still being pricked by its weaknesses. But I consider the weaknesses an opportunity for us to pursue a "more perfect" system.

The Thirteenth Amendment

Up to this point, we have discussed the foundational elements of our civil and criminal code and the biblical influences behind them. But just as the foundational governing documents include biblical elements that have been scarred by human sins, America's justice system has similarly been affected.

If we examine the eradication of slavery within the Thirteenth Amendment, we find that government officials created a carve-out that still allows the government to deprive some people of their inherent rights. Those people are criminals. Here is what we read in the Thirteenth Amendment:

> Neither slavery nor involuntary servitude, *except as a punishment for crime whereof the party shall have been duly convicted*, shall exist within the United States, or any place subject to their jurisdiction.[12]

Proponents of the criminal carve-out say that people who commit crimes are violating their implicit contract with the government and society. If they commit crimes, they do so with full knowledge that they can be punished. And, for that reason, they deserve to lose their privileges as citizens.

The fallacies of this argument are obvious. For one thing, slavery isn't just wrong until someone deserves it. It's wrong because it denies a person the dignity that is inherently due to them. And even if we can justify taking away someone's freedom or privileges because they are being punished for a crime, the goal of criminal justice must be to remove that person from society and reform their behavior, although the latter goal is undoubtedly missing from much of our current penal system.

Moreover, slavery is a means to a greedy end, and we should never allow the forced labor of criminals for the advancement of economic gain. In my view, this criminal carve-out provision in the Thirteenth Amendment still violates the spirit of the Constitution and our duty to honor the imago Dei.

Prison Labor

The question being debated today is whether slavery exists in America's current criminal justice system. I think most people will acknowledge that the incarcerated work in the prisons where they are held, but we may not agree that such work is slavery. This is a complicated issue, and I'll simply scratch the surface here. But I encourage you to do more research on this issue if you are inclined.

The Thirteenth Amendment was enacted in 1865, and by 1871, the Virginia Supreme Court declared that prisoners were "slaves of the State undergoing punishment for heinous crimes committed against the laws of the land."[13] In 1901, Mississippi opened a state penitentiary, Parchman, which was once a plantation. In the beginning, the inmates worked in the plantation fields, earn-ing the state nearly a six-figure income each year by 1905. That's the equivalent of about $5 million today. Court filings report that the prisoners were beaten with a 3-foot-long, 6-inch-wide whip named "Black Annie."[14] After decades of abuse, inmates filed a class-action lawsuit, and, in 1971, a federal court scolded Missis-sippi for its actions. The court stated that the prison committed "inhumanities, illegal conduct, and other indignities," and that the facilities were "unfit for human habitation."[15]

This example shows the relatively seamless transition between government-sanctioned slavery on plantations that became pris-ons. And while most prisons may not engage in the same types of illegal conduct as Parchman, problems still abound.

A 2022 report showed that two out of three people in state and federal prisons also work for the prison. More than 76 percent of these incarcerated workers surveyed by the Bureau of Justice Statistics said that they must work or they will be punished with solitary confinement, denial of reduced sentences, loss of family visitation, and other tactics.[16]

These incarcerated workers provide an economic value of over $2 billion per year in goods and $9 billion per year in ser-vices for prison maintenance. Because more than 80 percent of prison workers do maintenance work, they offset significant costs for the prison system. Another 8 percent of prison workers help with public works projects in parks, school grounds, cem-eteries, landfills, and in dozens of other ways.[17] Further, US law excludes incarcerated workers from workplace protections and safety guarantees.

And incarcerated workers earn little to no pay at all.[18] On average, incarcerated workers earn 13 to 52 cents per hour nation-wide. Seven states—Alabama, Arkansas, Florida, Georgia, Mississippi, South Carolina, and Texas—don't pay prison workers at all. The states that do pay their workers take upward of 80 percent of the wages for room and board, restitution, court costs, and other fees for building and sustaining the prisons. The prisons also charge inflated fees for phone calls, food, medical care, and hygiene products. As a result of the lack of ability to financially sustain themselves, families with incarcerated members spend $2.9 billion per year for commissary accounts and other expenses. More than half of states allow incarcerated workers to help with emergency operations for disasters and emergencies. Work for private companies accounts for less than 1 percent of incarcerated work assignments.[19]

There is room for much debate about whether the state should be able to use incarcerated individuals for labor. My belief is that while incarcerated individuals should be allowed to work, they should not be compelled to do so without compensation. This would allow those who are incarcerated to still provide for family members on the outside, which could only benefit society. The current system, which allows for forced labor under the Thirteenth Amendment, does not honor the divine identity of each person and, in essence, promotes a form of slavery.

Racial Disparities and Mass Incarceration

Michelle Alexander, author of *The New Jim Crow*, argues that America's criminal justice system, particularly its treatment of felons, is a refined version of segregationist America, in which blacks were denied basic rights.[20] While it would be difficult to tie all these issues to a deliberate scheme on the part of white suprema-cists, it is clear that her hypothesis relies on factual evidence.

Take, for instance, what happens to someone when he or she is marked as a felon. A felony is any crime that is punish-able with at least one year of jail time. That's it. The crime does not have to be violent or particularly heinous to warrant such a sentence. But to be a felon not only allows you to be used as a slave in the penitentiary, it also makes you ineligible for vot-ing, employment, housing, public programs, and much more. These are the very same rights denied to blacks for decades. I almost don't need to say that a disproportionate amount of peo-ple in prison and with felony records are black. Black men com-prise 6.5 percent of the US population yet represent 40 percent of the prison population.[21] And the likelihood of a white man going to prison in his lifetime is 1 in 17.[22] For a black man, the likelihood is 1 in 3.[23]

Thus, the face of the new carve-out for dehumanized treat-ment looks the same as it did during slavery and Jim Crow. This system is not necessarily one of racism, but rather, one of racial indifference.[24] That is, we know that the criminal justice system is swallowing up an entire race at an alarming rate, and rather than examine the problem and treat it, we tend to be indifferent because it does not impact us. Rather than seeing this reality as an indictment against whites, Alexander's arguments deserve care-ful consideration by Christians who believe that America must be a just society.

Once slavery was abolished, four million people were freed who were formerly considered property.[25] It should not surprise us that the first prison boom happened after slavery was abolished.

Blacks were arrested for petty crimes like loitering and vagrancy. Ultimately, the imprisoned blacks were used to rebuild the economy of the South, which took a severe hit after the free labor that accompanied slavery was outlawed.

During Jim Crow, civil rights advocates were portrayed in the media as criminals for violating segregation laws, even though their lunch-counter sit-ins and bus boycotts were not violent. When the Civil Rights Act was signed, crime rates were surging. Some think this was because baby boomers were entering adulthood. Whatever the reason, this led to a myriad of criminal policies meant to control the rising crime rates nationwide. In the 1970s, there were 357,000 people in America's prisons. This number would increase sevenfold in only a few decades.[26]

Richard Nixon's administration began a campaign to institute a war on crime, which included targeting all forms of drug offenses. John Ehrlichman, a Nixon advisor, reportedly admitted that the Nixon administration wanted to target hippies and blacks, so they criminalized marijuana and heroin, respectively. Regardless of the motivations, the prison population grew to more than 580,000 people by 1980.[27]

Undoubtedly, Ronald Reagan's war on drugs, declared in 1982, was the impetus to an era of mass incarceration. This is when Congress enacted drug laws with the varying minimum mandatory sentences for powder cocaine, crack cocaine, and other drugs. Politicians, TV personalities, and others, including blacks, advocated for harsher sentences on criminal convictions.

Throughout the 1980s, Republican politicians bragged about being tough on crime and won elections based at least partially on that rhetoric. By the early 1990s, the Democrats, most notably

Bill Clinton, adopted the tough-on-crime position in their plat-form. And by 1990, the prison population had ballooned to more than 1.1 million people.[28]

In the 1990s, the three-strikes rule emerged, often triggering life sentences for a third violent felony. The infamous 1994 Federal Crime Bill created a massive expansion of prisons and police forces throughout the nation. By the early 2000s, the prison population reached two million people.[29]

In 2025, a highly publicized article in *The New York Times* revealed there were 1.5 million black men from the prime-age years of 25 to 54 missing from daily life. The higher imprisonment rates of black men account for almost 600,000 of the missing million, with mortality accounting for the other portion. Almost 1 in 12 black men in this age group were behind bars, compared with 1 in 60 nonblack men in the same age group.[30]

While the racial disparities in the criminal justice system are alarming, mass incarceration has impacted all races. In 2014, the prison population was a whopping 2.3 million. Consider that America is home to about 5 percent of the world's population, but it has about 25 percent of the world's prisoners.[31]

Now, a natural counter for this information is that most of these incarcerated people did, in fact, commit crimes, and we can't blame a system for the actions of individuals. Most people are not being railroaded by the criminal justice system. The vast majority of those in prison committed the crimes they were convicted of. This doesn't excuse any injustices that may take place during the criminal process, but we must accept that, at minimum, the majority are guilty. This truth is often overlooked by criminal justice reform advocates. But when our prison population is compared to those of other countries, the numbers beg the question of whether America is over-penalizing its people.

Private Prisons

A private prison is a facility that incarcerates offenders for profit. The trend to privatize prisons began in 1984 when Hamilton County, Tennessee and Bay County, Florida contracted with the private sector to provide facilities for prisoners.[32] The shift from a publicly operated correctional system to a private one invokes concerns about the conflict between public and private interests. While the government should focus on inmate and staff safety, the private sector may be less concerned with the ethical or fair treatment of inmates. Instead, some argue, the private sector will likely hire the minimum number of staff necessary to supervise the maximum number of inmates in order to increase profits.[33]

But the private prison sector is relatively limited. While the private prison population increased by 14 percent since 2000, in 2020, private prisons accounted for only about 8 percent of the total state and federal prison population. While some states, like Montana, house about half of their inmates in private prisons, 22 states don't use private prisons at all.[34] Many have scolded the federal government for measures that incentivized private prisons and encouraged mass incarceration, but 90 percent of prisoners are in a state facility.[35]

Still, private prisons incentivize the government to imprison its citizens rather than to free them. Currently, private prisons earn more than $3 billion per year, with revenue deriving from lucrative contracts with federal and state governments.[36] The contracts include provisions that require states to hold a certain number of prisoners or the government must pay hefty fines.[37] A quota, which is sometimes as much as 90 percent of a prison facility's total capacity, produces an immoral incentive to imprison as many people as possible for as long as possible.[38]

Thus, if you want to contribute toward making changes to the way prisons are managed, whether by private or public entities, start by examining ways to make a difference in your home state. This includes being committed to voting in state and local elections, an often-neglected activity by most state residents. Across the country, only 15 to 27 percent of eligible voters vote in their local elections.[39]

Police Brutality

By far, much of the negative media scrutiny about our criminal justice system focuses on police brutality. This is a delicate subject that often sparks divisive political conversations. I want to explore one incident that incorporates several aspects of this conflict in one story.

In early 2020, Breonna Taylor was killed by police officers while they served a search warrant on her home. At the time, I had taken up creating educational videos about the law, and I did a deep dive into the case. What I found was remarkable. The media lied about important facts of the case. Now there should be some grace shown during the first day or two as all the facts are gathered, but even months later, the media continued to manipulate the facts.

Most of the media claimed that Taylor and her boyfriend, Kenneth Walker, were asleep in their beds when the police barged into the apartment. Allegedly, the police shot and killed Taylor without justification. As much as ten months later, this version of events was shared repeatedly by major media outlets and on social media.

The actual story—based on police reports and witness testimony—is very different indeed. Three Louisville police officers descended on Taylor's apartment to serve a search warrant. They claim they knocked, and a few neighbors said they heard the police pounding on Taylor's door. Walker said in a sworn statement that he heard the knocking but when he asked who it was, no one answered. Either way, this is already looking much different than the version we were initially fed by the media.

Walker said he and Taylor entered the hallway, and Walker was armed. The police barged through the door, and Walker opened fire on the officers, hitting one in the leg. In response, the officers fired more than 30 rounds. Taylor, who was unarmed and also in the hallway with Walker, was hit by six bullets and subsequently died. There are some who try to argue that Taylor was behind Walker when those shots were fired, but that seems almost impossible, considering she was shot six times and Walker was not shot at all. After the shooting, police footage shows that when the police asked Walker who fired the shots at the police, Walker said Taylor did.

After the incident, the media frenzy erupted and there were repeated calls for the officers involved in the shooting to be fired and even indicted. Taylor's family filed a wrongful death suit against Louisville, and the police department settled the suit. Eventually, the officers were indicted, but not for shooting Taylor. They were indicted for endangering others in her apartment building with their reckless, excessive shooting.

Now, I'll start by saying that a myriad of factors contributed to Taylor's death, and some of the blame lies squarely in the hands of the Louisville Metro Police Department. Approval of the no-knock warrant is just one decision in a series of others that contributed to the tragic shooting. But Walker's actions were also reckless, and some of the police evidence of Taylor posing in photos with drugs and guns implies that she may have been involved in illicit activities.

Taylor's shooting was the impetus for calls from the now-disgraced Black Lives Matter organization for defunding the police. After this, and subsequent publicized interactions between the police and civilians, many in the country turned on the nation's police forces, and many cities and states defunded their police departments. This decision resulted in a rise in crime.

False narratives about police brutality in the black community tend to produce skepticism on the part of whites and others. And many conservative commentators argue that these narratives are myths.

But the constant media barrage about black people being assaulted and killed by police officers have produced weariness, frustration, and anger in the black community, which is exacerbated by false narratives that often spread like wildfire, as happened with Taylor's death. And this impact on the black community is real even if the media is mischaracterizing the frequency of these events.

JUDGES: "PRESSURE IS A PRIVILEGE"

Judges are at the top of the justice pyramid. For this reason, Americans should pay close attention to the people who end up in this position. While judges may have a lot of training, they are still people who can be influenced by criticism. We should look for people who can resist the social pressure of being in the public eye. Judges should be divorced from such influence.

In 2023, federal appellate judge James Ho said in a speech, "Citizens have every right to expect federal judges to follow the law in every case, no matter how belligerent or baseless the booing of the crowd, because that's the job."[40] He said judges, much like Christians, should get comfortable with harsh criticism.

Even though judges should act independently of any criticism they might face, they should be generally aware of their critics' arguments. For one, judges should consider constructive criticism because it could sharpen their thinking. But they should also be discerning enough to differentiate between well-meaning criticism and comments that are meant to inappropriately influence or threaten the judiciary. For example, calls to reform or pack the courts are coercive rather than helpful.

In March 2024, in *Trump v. Anderson*, the justices struck down efforts by Democratic secretaries of state to remove Donald Trump from the 2024 presidential ballot. The states asserted that Trump violated the disqualification clause. Despite the political disharmony, the justices unanimously rejected the states' actions as a usurpation of Congress's power over federal elections.[41]

In response to the decision, *The Hill* published an op-ed that said, "Most Americans doubt that SCOTUS will be impartial in decisions affecting the 2024 election. By striking down Colorado's decision to remove Trump from the ballot, the justices validated their fears. Tragically we have lost faith in the court as the last, best stop in the pursuit of unencumbered justice. No wonder calls to reform it by adding justices are resurfacing."[42]

The op-ed also mentioned a bill that was reintroduced in the

Senate in March 2024 to increase the number of justices on the US Supreme Court from 9 to 13. This is called court packing, and it consists of adding seats to the federal courts and filling them with judges who will prioritize political rather than judicial ends. Court packing destroys the effectiveness of the court because the judges are appointed for the purpose of serving the political party that put them in power, rather the people.

Supporting improper assertions of power is advocating for tyranny. This sentiment is rooted in the desire to dismantle the foundation of American government and start anew. Law professors from Harvard and Yale have argued that the Constitution should be "radically" changed to "reclaim America from constitutionalism."[43] But America would not be free without the Constitution. Therefore, calls to dismantle it should be scrutinized.

Because judges swear an oath to defend and protect the Constitution, they should be a roadblock to tyranny. Perhaps the reason some people take the Constitution for granted is because they think it is designed to protect the government, but it's really designed to protect the people. Its foundation is rooted in timeless principles, and judges are obligated to preserve its power and intentions. As Americans, we should support only those judges who subscribe to these core principles of judicial philosophy.

But many people tend to support judges and politicians in general based on party affiliation or characteristics irrelevant to the fair exercise of law. I testified at the US Supreme Court confirmation hearings for Justice Ketanji Brown Jackson in early 2022. After a careful vetting, my firm decided she was not a justice we would want on the Supreme Court because of her radically liberal beliefs. Frankly, knowing about her beliefs, I couldn't see how most conservatives or Christians could support her. Those who back her, including pro-abortion and gay and transgender activists, are on her side because they know she will support their causes.

Jackson's speeches reveal that she supports same-sex unions.[44] My confirmation hearing testimony focused on Jackson's support for critical race theory, which we will unpack in more detail in the education chapter of this book. Suffice it to say, CRT cannot and will not lead to the improvement of our society, and it is a belief system that no justice should subscribe to.

I realized that most of the people who supported Justice Jackson had very little idea about who she was or what she believed. Sadly, many Christians fell into this category as well. They supported her solely because she would be the first black woman to sit on the high court, but race is not a reason to support anyone.

We must do our homework on candidates, especially because we are Christians. We should not allow the world to persuade us about who to support. We must have well-informed opinions about the people who desire to serve and represent us in our government. We often forget this, but those who work for the government—lawyers, senators, police officers, presidents, judges, and the like—are public servants. And they are accountable to God.

A SERVANT OF JUSTICE

Some people commit crimes out of desperation. Others commit crimes because of opportunity. And still others commit crimes as a lifestyle. We should accept that there are people in our society who will choose to be criminals. For this reason, we need law enforcement. Our society must value those who enforce the law, and no one knows that more than those who are victims of crime.

God is just. Only He knows how to achieve justice. As we survey our justice system, we often feel overwhelmed and assume there is little hope for change. While things are not perfect, we have come a long way in addressing justice issues in our country. We must continue to march forward, trusting that God can use our influence to help point others in the right direction.

On one hand, God stands in defense of the oppressed and the needy, the widow, the orphan, and the poor. They receive His help when they are wronged. His administration of justice for the wronged is an extension of His love and grace for those who call upon Him (Psalms 97:11-12; 112:3-6; 116:5; 118:15-19). At the same time, God does not spare the wicked (Ezekiel 7:4, 9, 27; 8:18; 9:10), and will ensure that they are punished for their wrongdoing.[45]

Likewise, as a society, we must see to it that those who violate the proper social order and harm or endanger those around them are punished appropriately and proportionately to the crime or tort committed. Our goal as Christians is to advocate for a justice system that achieves this balance of restorative and retributive justice. But we can do this only by following God's standards. God is the only lawgiver and judge (James 4:12).

On another note, the church is responsible for administering justice internally. We should ensure we provide the body with the tools to view the world accurately. This means that we hold leaders and members of our church accountable when they violate biblical principles. The church must keep watch and ensure that those who claim to walk with the Lord are following the Lord's precepts. We must hold those who proclaim the name of

Jesus Christ accountable, and not allow anyone to use His name to advocate for evil.

Church discipline is also retributive and restorative, mirroring God's process with His people. Based on the authority granted to the church, which is under Christ's rule, internal discipline is meant to maintain the integrity and purity of the church, to protect other believers from corruption, and to encourage spiritual maturity in the body.[46]

Overall, the church must be united internally so we can have an impact externally. If we want to maintain justice in our society, we must consistently and neutrally uphold God's standards. When we are united by God's standards, we will be united in our message to the world, we will be united when we minister to the world, and we will avoid being deceived by the world.

When we are united by God's standards, we will be united in our message to the world, we will be united when we minister to the world, and we will avoid being deceived by the world.

CHAPTER 9

LIBERATE EDUCATION

L aw students learn how to be lawyers by studying cases. I love reading cases because each one is a unique story about people whose lives inadvertently impacted the law. Each person involved becomes a witness for one side or the other, and ultimately, all the parties involved become witnesses for our justice system. Each case is a story about people in conflict and demonstrates how a court applies the law to solve the conflict. In essence, cases illustrate to lawyers how the courts administer justice.

One reason this practice of studying cases is so effective is because stories are powerful teachers. Stories frame information in a real-life context that helps to imprint the story and its lesson in our mind. When I was a child, I read lots of Aesop's fables. These simple and engaging stories were designed to teach deep life lessons. One of my favorites was "The Wolf in Sheep's Clothing."

In this fable, a wolf wanted to eat lamb, but it was difficult for him to catch one because of the watchfulness of their shepherd.

The wolf decided to disguise himself with sheepskin and roam among the flock. He eventually led some lambs away and ate them. But one day, it happened that the shepherd felt a hankering for some mutton stew. He killed the first lamb he captured, and it happened to be the wolf.

It is one thing for us to hear a lesson made in isolation; the evildoer often comes to harm through his own deceit.[1] But it is quite another for us to hear a story that illustrates the truth of the lesson. This is why, when Jesus spoke to His disciples, He used stories to illustrate principles in God's truth.[2] He knew His disciples, and all who heard the stories would remember the principles more easily if they were wrapped in a parable.

In one parable, Jesus tells us about the importance of forgiveness (Matthew 18:21-35). He illustrates how God wipes the debt of our sins clean with His forgiveness, which is made possible through the shed blood of Christ. In turn, He expects us to forgive others. In this parable, Jesus likens our state without Him to one who is overloaded with debt that she cannot repay. The story shows us the invaluable liberty offered by God's forgiveness, and His expectation that we, too, grant the gift of forgiveness to others.

The parable is also a reminder that we should not mistake God's instruction that we live in righteousness as a form of bondage or control. His request is not a restriction; in His view, it is vital for our liberation. There is no worse slavery than to live without God. By contrast, those who receive Christ as Savior become free from such bondage and live an abundant life. True liberation, in the Christian sense, is to be a slave to God, because where the spirit of the Lord is, there is liberty (2 Corinthians 3:17).

*We should not mistake God's instruction that we live
in righteousness as a form of bondage or control...
There is no worse slavery than to live without God.*

Jesus' methods should teach us that storytelling is useful, if not instrumental, for us to be like Him. As believers, we can teach others about Jesus by telling our own stories. Our stories are our testimonies of what we've experienced in the kingdom of God. And our testimonies are also powerful weapons against the kingdom of darkness (Revelation 12:11). God's desired fruit of our testimony is to raise up another disciple of Jesus Christ who finds God's gift of liberty.[3]

This truth contains a patriotic sentiment: America upholds a parallel belief that each of its citizens is entitled to make their own choices about religion and the kind of life they want to live. True liberation begins with our ability to think and reason and make informed choices and, if you are inclined, to be used by God to fulfill His purposes for your life.

Critical to both the spiritual and the secular decision-making processes is that we have knowledge of the options. For example, in Christianity, it is not just the truth that sets us free; rather, it is the truth *we know* that sets us free (John 8:32). In other words, being informed about the gospel is necessary before we can choose it.

In America, education equips children with knowledge about their options in life and provides them with the critical thinking skills needed to make the best decisions. This ensures our children will live a life of liberty. An education system that does not liberate, but instead, puts our children in bondage must be corrected before the bad fruit comes to harvest. We must be watchful of the seeds that we plant in the minds of our children and ensure that they will bear good fruit in the next generation.

A TEACHER TESTIFIES

I sometimes contemplate Jesus' statement that those who make themselves like little children are the greatest in the kingdom of heaven (Matthew 18:4). What is it about children that makes this so? Is it their innocence or joyful attitude? Perhaps it is because children tend to have a great amount of faith. Their imaginations are untainted by the limitations of human reason, and they more readily believe that God really can do the impossible.

In 2011, while I was still living in Atlanta, I joined Teach For America, a nonprofit organization dedicated to eliminating the achievement gap in education between low income (often minority) students and affluent white students. Prior to joining TFA, I worked in higher education for about four years. I joined TFA because I felt led to teach in a K-12 classroom.

Atlanta Public Schools assigned me to work with special education students, a population that is always short of teachers. It was a difficult assignment because the students not only had intellectual disabilities, but they were also diagnosed with behavioral disorders. My assigned classroom was self-contained, meaning it would only include students with behavioral disorders who were no longer permitted in a general education classroom. Adding to the challenge was the fact I would have to teach all subjects to fourth and fifth graders in one classroom.

I never thought about teaching before God compelled me to do so, and I felt inadequate for the task. But I dove in and prayed about how I could reach students who were deficient in academics and self-control. Most of the students were at least two or three grade levels below fourth and fifth grade reading levels. One fifth grade student was barely reading at a kindergarten level. She was still unable to identify some letter sounds.

After much prayer, I felt that my true assignment was not only to ensure the students' academic progress but also teach them that they were worthy of academic success. My goal would be to make them want to be successful. After years of being disciplined, failing tests, and facing ridicule from peers, many of the students lacked self-esteem. I knew this was the first thing I had to tackle.

I spent the first few weeks of school building a strong classroom culture. The students set goals and identified family members, coaches, and friends whom they wanted to make proud. We posted their visions on the wall, and I asked them to commit to working hard to achieve their goals. They did.

What happened over that school year could only be described as a miracle. I, as a first-year teacher, led these students to grow nearly three years of reading in one year. The average is 0.7 years. None of the students had ever passed a state proficiency test, but 80 percent of my students passed reading that year, and more than half passed math.

But the most satisfying part of that experience was the character development I witnessed in my students. Children who formerly yelled, attacked classmates, ripped papers, threw books, shoved desks, and even ran out of the classroom and the school building now exercised self-control and built amicable relationships with their classmates. All the students were diagnosed with ADHD, but they were focused and able to complete assignments throughout the day. They were different children.

The experience changed me as much as it changed my students. It was one of the first times I felt God work through me to impact someone else's life. I knew that because of the students' diagnoses and academic deficiencies at the beginning of year, those students were on the road to a dismal life. The statistics were not in their favor and demonstrated that it was likely they would end up in prison if something did not change. I believe that what God did through me in that classroom set those students on a different life path.

This experience also demonstrated for me that an education or the lack thereof can make or break a person. An insufficient education can limit a student's life choices because they are unaware of their options, incapable of critically thinking their way out of difficult situations, or because their intellectual limitations hindered their access to higher education or entrepreneurial options.

Depending upon how it is used, education has a paradoxical nature in that it serves to either liberate or oppress.[4] Our growth as a society depends on our education system. We want to create citizens who can contribute to our intellectual elevation and social development. Many of the capacities that we take for granted—like rational judgment and critical thinking—are historically emergent and are reliant upon the continuation of a high-quality education.[5]

This is not to say that everyone needs a higher education to succeed, but it is obvious that a primary-level education is foundational.

While many people succeed with a limited education, some dropping out as early as middle school, the vast majority of people will not succeed without adequate critical thinking skills and, at the very least, literacy.

Pedagogy is the art of creating liberated citizens, which is the true mark of a democratic education system, especially a system that rests on Christian ideals. Our culture must embrace this truth to support the structure upon which true pedagogy needs to operate. Our culture must become one that is dedicated to our continued improvement as a citizenry to produce highly educated, liberated individuals who can improve and correct our world. We can do this effectively only by believing—or at least behaving as if we believe—that all individuals have an inherent worth and the ability to contribute to our society.

AMERICA'S REPORT CARD

School is the first impression children get of society.[6] Consider what the following statistics indicate: As of 2022, American students rank twenty-eighth in math, compared to other students in 27 industrialized countries.[7] About a third of students in elementary school are behind on reading and only 36 percent of fourth graders are proficient at grade-level math.[8] As of 2022, only 13 percent of students were proficient in American history.[9]

The statistics regarding minority and low-income students are even more disheartening. Eighty percent of lower-income fourth graders do not read at their grade level, compared to 49 percent of their wealthier peers.[10] Blacks and Latinos are also twice as likely as whites to not graduate from high school.[11]

These disparities also exist in school discipline practices and further lead to America's failure to produce liberated citizens. Studies show that African-American students are far more likely than their white peers to be suspended, expelled, or arrested for the same kind of conduct at school.[12] Forty percent of students expelled from school are black, and 70 percent of students involved in in-school arrests or referred to law enforcement are black or Latino.[13] Oftentimes when kids are removed from school, they end up in inferior settings, such as suspension centers, alternative schools, and juvenile prisons.[14] Any child who cannot read proficiently by the end of the fourth grade has about a 78 percent chance of never catching up, and two-thirds of them will end up in jail or on welfare.[15]

America's education crisis is a major policy concern for our country that affects all other areas of public welfare. A recent Council on Foreign Relations Task Force on Education Reform and National Security concluded that the country's "educational failure puts the United States' future economic prosperity, global position, and physical safety at risk."[16]

The National Assessment of Educational Progress—often nicknamed the Nation's Report Card—provides the most comprehensive view of the state of American education available. Since 1992, it has given us a longitudinal record of where our students are and where they should go. Between 2012 and 2020, the achievement gap between black and white 13-year-olds grew by 7 points.[17]

In what follows, the word *basic* means the ability to understand words and answer simple questions about factual information that appears in text. In 2019, 34 percent of fourth graders were below basic reading level. Many couldn't read at all, and even more couldn't understand what they read. When we consider students who qualify for free and reduced-cost lunches, half are below basic reading level.[18] Only 24 percent of high school seniors have a reasonable knowledge of civics—the rights and duties of citizens in our republic.[19]

We can see that these gross disparities will have a greater impact on the country when we consider that, as of 2015, poor or low-income students make up the majority of the student population in the United States.[20] As the percentage of minority students grows, the US will be left with an education system that fails to serve the majority of its children properly, aggravating the education gaps.[21]

Some suggest that we should eliminate our system of standardized testing. Unfortunately, while testing is imperfect, it is the best of the options available to assess where students are education-wise.[22] When testing is done using an individualized approach, you will always know where a student is and what they need.[23] However, most American public school classrooms are not equipped with a teacher-student ratio that makes an individualized approach possible with every student.

Regardless, lowering standards is not the way to address the problems. High expectations are essential for keeping students inspired and challenged, and for ensuring America can compete globally. Our goal must be to address why American education is failing our students. We should examine why students aren't passing their tests, not eliminate tests altogether. We should work to enable our children to meet the standards, not assume that they cannot meet the standards. President George W. Bush famously called out "the soft bigotry of low expectations."[24]

THE SCHOOL-TO-PRISON PIPELINE

The school-to-prison pipeline is one of America's greatest shames. The term *school-to-prison pipeline* refers to a process by which youth who experience punitive punishment in schools are increasingly enmeshed within the criminal justice system.[25]

In *The New Jim Crow*, Michelle Alexander argues that the racial caste system that we worked to abolish during the civil rights movement has evolved.[26] This system, she argues, now functions through the criminal justice process[27] and enslaves minorities and the poor through mass incarceration.[28] We explored this argument in the context of justice.

And while my argument is not necessarily focused on a system but the people who are working in it, I agree that there are racial-related issues in the criminal justice system. But based on my research and experiences as a teacher, I believe that public schools are the classroom of indoctrination that significantly impacts a student's involvement with the criminal justice system.

While the school-to-prison pipeline focuses on the disciplinary practices of districts, which treat students as criminals while they are still children, I believe the real indoctrination goes much deeper than discipline. Eight-five percent of juvenile offenders have problems reading, and three out of every five individuals in America's prisons cannot read at all.[29] Of all the males in state prison, 68 percent do not have a high school diploma.[30] The lack of academic training also makes children susceptible to resorting to criminal activity in order to make a living. This reveals how much today's schools contribute to desperation, or at least a lack of critical thinking about how to make a legal living.

While teaching in Atlanta Public Schools, I spoke to students who believed that going to jail and having a "baby mama" was a normal way of living. Some students in the fifth grade ridiculed another student who revealed her family did not use food stamps. While these issues can impact students of any race and demographic, it was revelatory that many of them considered these issues to be normal. And thus, the students expected these circumstances to happen in their lives. These are powerful, and not necessarily preferential, self-fulfilling prophecies for young people to possess.

We need to educate students so that they can eventually contribute to society. Citizens must not only know the letter of the law, but also understand why it is reasonable.[31] Our goal should be to value all children enough to educate them adequately. We must consider the unique needs of students so we can find ways to instruct them effectively. Instead, we are creating generations of minds who are warped by inadequate and oppressive schooling and are unable to effectively participate in democratic discourse.[32]

We must also examine existing school-discipline policies, the practices of administrators, and the impact of those policies and practices on our children. Discipline choices that include punishment that removes students from the learning environment or puts them in an inferior one should never be utilized. This type of punishment is counterproductive to pedagogy because the purpose is to produce a liberated citizen who will be able to contribute to the economic and social growth of our society, and removing students from a proper learning environment will never achieve that end. We must commit to disciplinary practices intended to reform behavior rather than exacerbate the problems or destroy the student's ability to continue his or her education.

In general, the fact that our schools are becoming a channel for prison is a sounding alarm that we have discounted and discarded students instead of committing to liberating pedagogy. Frederick Douglass provides a sobering reminder for us in his declaration that it is easier to build strong children than to repair broken men.[33]

CRITICAL RACE THEORY

When I taught my students in Atlanta Public Schools, one reason I spent the first few weeks building the culture was because many of the students had destructive ways of thinking about themselves and the world. If I wanted to teach them anything, I had to start by dismantling and rebuilding their worldviews and the way they looked at themselves.

For most of their lives, my students were taught to believe, by explicit direction and through observation, that being black would be a handicap for them. They were convinced that being a part of the black race meant living in impoverished environments, being dependent on government assistance, going to jail, having babies out of wedlock, and other destructive habits. They discussed these issues with me openly, and there was no doubt that they believed it all to be true. My goal was to show them that their futures were not set in stone, and they could, in fact, do almost anything they put their minds to.

The beliefs my students had adopted are the foundational sentiments of critical race theory (CRT). The students didn't know the name of this theory. In fact, most people who ascribe to it don't know what they are ascribing to, but the damage is done nonetheless. I know CRT is a destructive form of thinking to introduce to students because I have seen its effects up close and personal.

CRT argues that racism is not a conscious individual decision or belief, but rather, a systemic problem created by American society and advanced primarily through the legal system. Consequently, CRT presupposes that the societal structure should be dismantled and rebuilt.[34]

This philosophy is antithetical to biblical conclusions. Racism is not an abstract concept that exists outside of human beings. It is advanced by people who act based on supremacist views and ignorance. And there is nothing to be gained by advancing CRT because it does not create a workable system for change. Dismantling the entire societal structure through implicit bias training and convincing white people that they are inherently racist because America has made them so is a losing tactic.

Moreover, CRT does nothing to empower black people to accept that they can succeed and advance in society regardless of the racist attitudes of the individuals they encounter. Racism may cause obstacles along the way but, for most, it will not be outcome determinative in our lives. Given what a CRT-like attitude produced in my students, I can tell you that it only produces despair, apathy, and resentment.

The only way we can effectively tackle racism is by encouraging individuals to take responsibility for how they behave, and they will do that only when they truly honor the intrinsic, divine value of every human being regardless of race. Racism is first and foremost a spiritual problem, and it must be solved spiritually. Interestingly, even Michelle Alexander has resigned herself to accepting that her observations about the criminal justice system and its problems can only be solved with spiritual principles.[35] She said,

This is not simply a legal problem, or a political problem, or a policy problem. At its core, America's journey from slavery to Jim Crow to mass incarceration raises profound moral and spiritual questions about who we are, individually and collectively, who we aim to become, and what we are willing to do now.[36]

Further, because of CRT's unbiblical origins, it embraces all sorts of ideas that are detrimental to the family in every community, including abortion and same-sex relationships. These ideas are not to be propagated in an education system that seeks to produce students who will continue to advance a free and productive republic. But currently, our education system is producing mentally, emotionally, and spiritually enslaved students. We must liberate, not liberalize, education.

Racism is first and foremost a spiritual problem, and it must be solved spiritually.

THE SEXUALIZATION OF CHILDREN

Filmmakers Mark and Amber Archer spent 14 months making *The Mind Polluters* so people could know what's happening in their children's schools. "No one wants to believe that our children are being groomed," Mark says in the movie's opening. "If we acknowledge it, we'll have to do something about it."

I was invited to a screening of the movie in 2022. It was eye-opening but not surprising. At the time, I was the leader of the education department at First Liberty, and people all over the country sent me samples of curricula, sex education programs, and library books that would make a porn star blush. I knew what was happening, but this movie did a precise job of describing how it was taking place.

The documentary explains the origins and impact of comprehensive sex education and the social-emotional learning standards promoted throughout the country. One of the educators in the documentary, Monica Cline, taught sex education to adolescents for ten years. Cline revealed that the training she received from Planned Parenthood did not focus on biology nor promote abstinence. Instead, it teaches adolescents how to be sexually active, where to go for disease testing, and where to get the "inevitable abortion."[37]

These are facts that parents of school-age students should be aware of. Most notably, you should know about a man named Alfred Kinsey. Kinsey attempted to change how adults viewed children by conducting pedophilic experiments on children to "prove" that children are sexual from birth. In his 1948 book *Sexual Behavior in the Human Male*, there is an infamous chart called "Table 34," where Kinsey documents the so-called orgasms of male children from five months old to 14 years old as they were being molested by adults.[38] Kinsey was trying to prove that children were sexual beings who desired and should engage in sexual behavior, even with adults.

In the 1997 biography *Alfred C. Kinsey: A Public/Private Life*, a former Kinsey coworker, James H. Jones, wrote that Kinsey "was determined to use science to strip human sexuality of its guilt and repression" and "undermine traditional morality." Jones admitted that Kinsey "spent his every waking hour attempting to change the sexual mores and sex offender laws of the United States."[39] Kinsey's advocacy led to revisions to the penal code in the 1950s, which decriminalized adultery, homosexuality, bestiality, and other sexual crimes.[40]

Many are ignorant of Kinsey's philosophies. He continues to be treated as a hero and brilliant scientist, as evident in a 2004 movie about Kinsey.[41] In 2022, Indiana University celebrated the seventy-fifth anniversary of the Kinsey Institute by unveiling a statue of Kinsey. At the ceremony, the university president, Pamela Whitten, said, "Around the nation and around the world, the Kinsey Institute is the trusted source for information on critical issues in human sexuality, relationships, gender and reproduction, and its reputation for excellent, relevant scholarship bolsters Indiana University's reputation."[42]

Kinsey's warped and demonic philosophy helped create the foundation for comprehensive sexual education programs used in today's schools. It also led states to pass laws that include exemptions on showing children obscene material if it happens in an "educational" setting. Sexually explicit material that would otherwise be unlawful is available to minors in public schools and libraries via "obscenity exceptions." Attempts to overturn such laws have largely been unsuccessful, even in states like Texas, with its Republican-led legislature.[43]

And the culture continues to push inappropriate sexual material upon children. In 2022, Governor Phil Murphy of New Jersey tried to pass an explicit sex education curriculum. The curriculum, written in secret, teaches six-year-olds about gender identity and encourages teachers to share with nine-year-olds a website that discusses pornography. The outrage was so swift and severe that Murphy recanted his support for the curriculum.[44]

In a stunning op-ed in *The Atlantic*, Conor Friedersdorf writes about the National Association for the Education of Young Children, which published a Code of Ethical Conduct that directs teachers to "acknowledge families' childrearing values and their right to make decisions for their children." The op-ed discusses a case study about how teachers should handle situations where the parent's beliefs about gender identity conflict with the child's. The study concluded that the teacher should defer to the child, not the parent. The author of the op-ed calls the 2019 case study "illuminating" because of its assertions that educators are morally obligated to overrule parents on a matter as fundamental as a child's gender.[45]

This article reflects the ongoing battle for parental rights in sex education. In Virginia, Glenn Youngkin ran for governor vowing to respect parental rights in public education. In keeping with that promise, Virginia released new education guidelines in 2023 "requiring that teachers obtain written permission from parents before beginning to treat students as transgender."

Friedersdorf claims that the moral obligation of Virginia's teachers are in conflict with the state law, which requires them to honor parental choices regarding gender identity. The article and the culture assume that affirming the feelings of a child regarding their gender is the right thing to do. This is a huge problem for the moral compass of society and the integrity of the law.

But there is a deeper issue buried in society's attempts to train children to follow their whims. Such an ideology also teaches children to bow to the whims of adults because of the obvious power advantage that adults have over children. Adults whose whims are in contradiction to Christianity teach children to detest it. The goal is to get the next generation to accept what was formerly unacceptable.

Mary Harrington, a UK-based writer who runs the Reactionary Feminist substack, writes, "Normophobia frames everything conventional, average, given, assumed, traditional, and normative—whether its origin be physiological or cultural—as arbitrarily and coercively constructed to support vested interests, particularly those of white, Christian, heterosexual men." Harrington says the purpose of "Drag Pedagogy," then, is "to redirect education from the formation of children to the inculcation of a reflexive distaste for physiological, social, and institutional norms of every kind; in other words, to the creation of the next generation of normophobes."[46]

This ideology denies basic truth. We should fight this ideal and be clear that it is morally wrong. We should know that these truths govern our nature. Natural laws will always prevail over incorrect ideology because the consequences of disobeying natural laws are unavoidable. This is the case whether people decide to become Christian or not. Natural laws govern everyone whether we believe them or not.

Even Harrington, who has no allegiance toward Christianity, acknowledges this truth when she says, "We may lament the Christianity-shaped hole in our discourse, but just because much of modern culture is post-Christian doesn't mean we no longer have a nature."[47]

The doctrine that supports the sexualization of children exists to feed the flesh. Children are being taught how to feel and not to think. Ultimately, our nation's public schools regard truth as antiquated, and we must act quickly to turn the tide.

A CURRICULUM FOR A
LIBERATED EDUCATION

Frustrated by 50 years of political inaction on the prohibition of alcohol, Frances Willard experimented with the school system. In the late 1870s, she created an anti-alcohol curriculum for the nation's third graders. She used it in many states. And, in a generation, pro- hibition was passed not just as a law but as a constitutional amend- ment. Willard proved that the American school system could steer the country—with a generational lag—in any direction that educa- tional leaders wanted it to go.[48] Progressives understand this lesson and are currently using the education system to push their agendas.

Christians must also understand this lesson and learn to use, as much as they can, the American educational system to push God's kingdom agenda. If America wants to provide a liberated education to its students, it must teach morals, literacy, and com- mit to integrating students with classmates of other cultures and ways of life, and provide rigorous, challenging pedagogy.

A proper education must first teach students morals, specifically core Christian virtues. For those who would argue that such an education is not appropriate under America's Establishment Clause, I would point you to the long history of Christianity being taught in public schools prior to this century. The Supreme Court clari- fied the true meaning of the Establishment Clause in the last few years after centuries of it being used to eradicate religion from the public sphere. It is without question an appropriate practice for the government to teach students the virtues that were the bed- rock of forming the country. This also includes teaching students that it is wrong to violate those virtues—which is how a nation can end up with immoral practices like slavery.

A foundational basis for this would include theism and the idea that we are one nation under God. And requiring students to read and learn about why the imago Dei compels us to treat people with a certain level of respect and dignity will only lead to a better social environment.

Even for those who do not accept Christianity as their own chosen religion, students will benefit from understanding America's Christian roots. Our current culture is full of students whose public education was devoid of such teachings, and the fruit has been young people who do not understand tolerance at all, even though they constantly scream about it.

And today's younger generations are losing the concept of patriotism, which is vital if we want to continue living in a free republic. The current education system's trend toward demonizing America will cause the future to be full of people who despise their country, and, consequently, will not want to preserve what makes it unique compared to other countries. And there is no question that freedom is rare in this world; it is not the norm. Our posterity must understand that though the country is flawed, we are still blessed to live in one of the few countries that has more freedoms than most others. We can aim to improve our nation and preserve it at the same time. But a healthy sense of patriotism means our patriotism never becomes idolatry.

With a moral foundation in place, we must then provide students with the skills to succeed and contribute to society. Besides today's moral deficiencies, my biggest concern for our public schools is that too many students are illiterate. Illiterate children will have fewer choices for their future, and, as statistics prove, the educational bondage of illiteracy increases the likelihood of literal bondage in prison.

We must make every effort to address the literacy problems in our schools. It doesn't make sense that students who attend school regularly aren't able to read. And while many people will say that a child's difficult home life is the reason we have so many failing students, I want to challenge that. Even when a student's home life is tough, a student who spends his entire day, five days a week, in school should at least learn how to read, regardless of what happens at his house. I cannot be convinced of otherwise. This is because I have taught students who had difficult home lives, some with little to no parental involvement, and they all left my classroom knowing how to read. There really is no excuse.

SCHOOL CHOICE MEANS EDUCATIONAL FREEDOM

School choice will help produce the kind of competition within school systems that increases the quality of the education that public schools are offering. Former Secretary of the Department of Education Betsy DeVos calls this "education freedom." Those who oppose school choice argue that it mostly helps the rich or the whites who want to flee from integrated schools. This is wildly inaccurate, as school choice provides students in low-performing schools with the ability to attend high-performing schools outside of their neighborhoods.

And, as is true in almost any market, when you give the public the ability to choose, it naturally elevates the standards for the providers in that market. Many people have complained that school choice, especially options that allow parents to send their children to religious schools using public funding, are a threat to public schools. But if public schools want to keep students enrolled, then all they have to do is meet a higher standard.

Oftentimes, public schools are enabled in their poor performance because there is no consequence for their disappointing academics. They still receive funding, and thus there is no incentive for the school or district to make changes to address the problems.

More than that, school choice is associated with higher achievement levels and gains.[49] The fact is that providing parents and students with school choice improves the quality of education that students receive. There is no reason not to offer this option in every state and every school district in America.

There are many different expressions of school choice, but one of the most popular is charter schools. These are public, tax-payer-funded, tuition-free schools that are open to any student who wants to attend. Enrollment is usually done through a lottery system because these schools usually have waiting lists. Charter schools are different than a traditional public school because they are not run by the government and are often free from government restrictions and mandates that apply to traditional public schools. The creative approaches used by charter schools leads to improved educational outcomes.[50]

The research is unanimous that charter schools produce high-performing students. For example, Success Academy is a charter school district in New York and the number one performing district in the state. Between 2011 and 2016, the rigor at the school provided students with the equivalent of 137 days of extra learning in reading and an astounding 237 days of math instruction versus New York's public schools.[51] Students who attend charter schools in Detroit gain about three months of added learning each year versus their assigned public schools.[52] This means that students at charter schools attend classes the same number of days as those at a traditional public school, but learn exponentially more in that time.

Charter schools are also more efficient with their use of public dollars. On average, charter schools receive 16 percent less funding than traditional public schools.[53] And charter schools in major cities across the country receive about 33 percent less funding than traditional public schools.[54] Consequently, charter schools are much more efficient with the school day and the public dollar than government-run public schools. These statistics provide compelling proof that every state needs more charter schools.

An article in the *New York Times* discussed the popularity of charter schools in New York City. The article transparently stated that the "vast majority of students in charters are Black or Latino," and that charter schools "receive less per-pupil funding than district schools" and "typically outperform district schools in math and reading on state standardized tests." Despite these statistics, Democrats and teachers' unions oppose lifting the cap on charter schools in New York.[55]

At one point, both Democrats and Republicans supported charter schools through four presidential administrations.[56] But under President Biden, the bipartisan support diminished. Biden's administration called for banning some charter schools altogether and created rules that made it more difficult for charter schools to receive funding.[57]

Another option for school choice is magnet schools, which I happen to know a lot about because I attended a magnet high school in Florida. Magnet schools are also public, tuition-free schools, but they are structured around an academic or extracurricular theme. For example, most focus on STEM (science, technology, engineering, math), and others focus on vocational training, social sciences, the performing arts, and more.

Students must apply and be accepted to these schools. Magnet schools are effective at creating diverse student bodies because regardless of where these schools are located, parents want their children to attend because of their educational focus and reputation. This means that even if a school is located in a low-income area, it will attract students from outside of the neighborhood.[58] I will note that even though these schools are often integrated, the classrooms are sometimes not.

Another option is homeschooling, which continues to grow in popularity with the increasingly secular and godless nature of public schools. The biggest downside to homeschooling is that parents bear the costs of schooling, and they still pay taxes that go toward public schools even though their children don't attend them.

Other options for school choice rely on the idea that government funding should follow the student, not the district or the school. Education savings accounts are funds deposited into an account that a student can use to pay tuition or other education-related expenses. And then there are vouchers, or government funding that can be used to attend any school a student wants. Finally, tax-credit scholarships rely on individuals to make donations to nonprofits, and those organizations provide scholarships to students who need them to attend private schools.[59]

At the very least, all states should offer public school choice and allow students to choose any public school rather than being assigned to a school based on geography. While some states restrict these options to certain zones or districts, students should be able to attend any school in the state, although this may limit transportation options for the family.[60]

All of these are exceptional options, and every state should utilize one or all of these to encourage higher academic outcomes for all students. Of course, most states allow private schools to operate, but some erect barriers so that not all students can access them.

School choice remains a controversial subject and is often rejected by Democrats, who claim that it will destroy government-run public schools. But this argument demonstrates that there must be something wrong with public schools if they are afraid they will lose students to independently run public schools or private schools. The goal of schools is to provide a rigorous education, and any schools that are not doing that should not be serving students, no matter who runs them.

It would behoove Democrats to take a closer look at their position on this issue. When Ron DeSantis ran for reelection against Tallahassee mayor Andrew Gillum, DeSantis made school choice a primary part of his platform. Gillum, on the other hand, explicitly rejected school choice. Despite the fact Gillum is black, DeSantis secured 18 percent of the vote of black women compared to the national average for Republicans of 7 percent. Nearly 100,000 black women who normally vote Democrat voted for DeSantis in that election. DeSantis also secured 44 percent of the Latino vote.[61] And most attribute the surprising victory of Virginia governor Glenn Youngkin to his parental rights platform. These are decisive examples of how important educational matters are to the country, and they demonstrate why politicians should take educational issues more seriously.

THE KINGDOM MUST BE EDUCATED

Christianity is more than a religion; it is a kingdom. Our goal should be to continue strengthening that kingdom.[62] The Bible encourages us to train up children in the proper way so that when they are older, they will not depart from that training (Proverbs 22:6). Well, that truth works whether we are training our children in good or evil. Children become adults who apply their beliefs and abilities to whatever industry they end up in. If we continue to stand by and let the culture dumb down our children, we will face huge consequences in society and in the church.

The Bible encourages us to train up children in the proper way so that when they are older, they will not depart from that training (Proverbs 22:6).

While many Christians attempt to avoid the pitfalls of public education by putting their children into private religious schools, still, 90 percent of today's students attend public schools. That majority will be voting, serving in governments, running private companies, and working in the criminal justice system. Christians, as well as everyone else, will have to deal with the consequences of people who are the fruit of a subpar, immoral public education. The church must make educational issues a priority.

One way to do this is by keeping up with your state's educational initiatives. Some parental rights groups monitor these bills and summarize them on their websites. When you find initiatives that are concerning, flag them for your church community and rally together to oppose them by writing letters or signing petitions. Don't give up the minds of the American children without a fight.

CHAPTER 10

SPEAK AND RECOGNIZE TRUTH

The Spirit of the Lord sent Ezekiel to the middle of a valley full of dry bones (Ezekiel 37:1-2). God asked Ezekiel if the dry bones could live, and Ezekiel replied that only the Lord knew the answer (verse 3). The Lord directed Ezekiel to prophesy to the bones and tell them to grow tendons, flesh, and skin (verses 4-6). Before Ezekiel finished his prophecy, the bones began to rattle. He watched as they came together (verses 7-8).

The Lord then told Ezekiel to "prophesy to the breath" to breathe life into the slain bones. Ezekiel spoke, and breath entered the bones, and the bodies stood on their feet. The once-lifeless bones became a vast army (verses 9-10).

The Lord said that the bones "are the people of Israel," and he commanded Ezekiel to revive the people with the word of the Lord, like he did with the bones (verses 11-14). And once the resurrection of Israel was done, Israel would know who the Lord was (verses 13-14).

The Bible uses powerful stories like this to remind us how influential words can be. In this case, speaking the word of the Lord transformed a valley of dry old bones into an army. Similarly, the words we speak can have great influence. James 3 compares the power of speech to a bridle on a horse. By controlling the horse's mouth, you can control its direction (James 3:3). Likewise, a man who controls his mouth is able to control the course of his life. In fact, the Bible says that a man who controls his speech "is *perfect*, able to keep their whole body in check" (James 3:2).

Perfect.

In other words, if you can control your mouth, you can control your actions. The wise among us will see this as quite the incentive to watch everything that comes out of our mouths (Psalm 141:3; Proverbs 16:23). The power of the tongue is twofold: It can do both good and harm (Proverbs 18:21). James warns that our mouths can do a lot of damage. Like a match in a forest, your mouth can set fire to the course of your life (James 3:5-6).

Jesus warned us that it is what we say that defiles us, while also showing us the miracles a faith-filled word can produce. Jesus built His ministry with His words. The power of His speech drew in His followers and set aflame the anger of His enemies.

Throughout history, leaders have used the power of words to persuade and inspire people to action. Martin Luther King Jr., Nelson Mandela, John F. Kennedy, Barack Obama, Donald Trump, Benito Mussolini, and Adolf Hitler all demonstrated the enormous power of a skilled orator—for better or worse.

HISTORICAL PROPAGANDA

"It was a bright cold day in April, and the clocks were striking thirteen."[1]

The opening of the novel *Nineteen Eighty-Four* is memorable and haunting. The all-seeing Big Brother used technology to watch and control the population of Oceania. The government controlled the flow of information, rewriting history before disseminating it to the public to ensure they believed only what the government wanted. Eventually, the public's perception was distorted, and they could no longer recognize departures from reality. The clocks "striking thirteen," an impossibility, was an accepted reality in this dystopian society.

If you want to control someone, you must first control their speech. If you want someone to believe a lie and act on that lie, you must first convince them to speak the lie. This is part of the truth that Jesus articulated when He said we are defiled by what comes out of our mouths (Matthew 15:11).

Earlier, we examined how the Rwandan government used radio programs to demonize the Tutsi people so that it could convince the public that the Tutsis needed to be exterminated. The propaganda was so powerful that 800,000 Tutsis were slaughtered in the period of only a few months.

In the Soviet Union, the road to Communism began with Marxists infesting the culture with rhetoric about a revolution against the rich (or the capitalists) in the name of the working and poor in order to redistribute wealth.[2] The messages appealed to young intellectuals who despised the status quo and wanted to reorder society.[3] The ideas spread and celebrities and academics advocated for them, spreading them like wildfire and demonizing anyone who didn't subscribe to them. This started about two decades before Communism took hold of Russia.[4]

And the most famous tyrant of them all, Adolf Hitler, rose to power not just because he pursued it, but because the Germans gave it to him.[5] Hitler's success happened in part because he understood the power of language. Let's back up a bit and observe how Hitler achieved his goal.

The 1919 Treaty that ended World War 1 had 440 clauses, and 414 of them were devoted to punishing Germany. In the face of overwhelming defeat, the German people had no joy and no peace—only humiliation and suffering.[6] Politically, the country was in chaos. Money was worthless. Vigilantes ruled the streets. Berlin was a swamp of depravity. Everything and everyone was for sale. Self-proclaimed saviors seized the opportunity, appearing everywhere and declaring that they were sent by God to help. In German, there is no plural word for savior. There can be only one.[7]

Hitler first appeared on the scene around 1923 at a nationalist rally. Two months later, he tried to take over Germany as "the Munich savior" but failed. In 1929, Hitler led the national socialist party rally. An estimated 100,000 people attended and were entranced by his messages. At this point, the people wanted a revolution. They could choose candidates from the Communists or the Nazis. In March 1932, Hitler ran for president. He received 11 million votes in the election, and lost.

Most assumed this was the end of Hitler. But in less than a year, Hitler became chancellor. Eleven million people tuned in to a broadcast and listened to him talk about the purpose of politics. He said it must overcome division and be used for the greater good of the "rich and poor; educated and ignorant. In our hands alone lies the destiny of the German people."[8] The speech ignited Nazi party membership requests. In two weeks, Hitler would control Germany.

On February 27, 1933, there was a fire in Berlin at Germany's parliament building. Hitler used the disaster as an opportunity to blame the Communists, invoking people's fear against them. Within 24 hours of the fire, the freedoms of the press, expression, and public assembly were suspended. Within days of the fire, thousands of Communists were arrested. Hitler justified the changes in the government by saying it was necessary to rid the country of the Communists. By March 1933, many of the Communists were in jail, and the Nazi majority in the parliament voted to consolidate all power in Hitler. He was chancellor for only 52 days before he became a dictator.[9]

During the second half of 1933, 100,000 Germans were arrested. At least 600 were murdered in police custody, and people were beaten to induce fake confessions. Anyone who distanced themselves from the Nazis or opposed them was tortured with steal whips and electric drills. For everyone else, life was normal.[10]

And, at first, most Jewish people were convinced that no harm would come to them. But not long after Hitler became dictator, the government sent a message to the people to avoid all Jewish shops; buy only German. The Nazis boycotted all Jewish businesses in Germany. Fewer than 1 in 100 Germans were Jewish, but Hitler said the Jews were responsible for Germany's misfortunes.[11]

By February 1934, Hitler demanded absolute obedience to the Nazi party, and loyalists were assembled in Munich for an oath-taking ceremony. They were all there to swear their steadfast loyalty and absolute obedience to Hitler. They learned the mandatory German greeting: Heil Hitler. If you didn't use the greeting, you risked being sent to a concentration camp. In public, everyone was a Nazi, everyone did the salute, everything was watched, and everyone feared the next person was an informer.[12]

By 1934, the country's slogan was "one people, one realm, one leader." Hitler delivered a speech and addressed the "Jewish problem." He said it was time to find a legislative solution. By law, Jews were no longer considered German citizens. Marriage and sex between Germans and Jews was outlawed. By 1938, Hitler was already infamous in America. He was *Time* magazine's "man of the year."[13]

We all know what happened in the years to follow. Millions of Jewish people were murdered by Hitler's regime. And Hitler's words were the source of his power.

MODERN MEDIA

The use of language to control and manipulate people continues today, with China being the chief offender globally. Freedom House ranked China last in internet freedom out of 65 countries. In 2016, Reporters Without Borders ranked China 176 out of 180 countries in press freedom.[14] This makes China's government one of the world's most restrictive in terms of dictating communication practices.

The Council on Foreign Relations reported that President Xi Jinping's regime increased media censorship in 2016 with a decree regarding party and state news outlets: "All the work by the Chinese Communist Party's media must reflect the party's will, safeguard the party's authority, and safeguard the party's unity." The CCP mandated that all media must be supportive of the party's "thought, politics, and actions." The party heavily monitors and enforces its policies, relying on lawsuits, arrests, and other penalties to threaten journalists and media outlets. The Council of Foreign Relations reports that China imprisoned 38 journalists in 2017.[15]

China blocks many American apps like Facebook, Instagram, and others. China was in a heated battle with Google over its warning that China censored Google's search results. Google eventually retreated from the fight and dropped the warning, but the conflict highlighted China's oppressive communications style to the world.[16] China went further and eventually banned Gmail, a move that attracted the attention of the US State Department.[17]

While China's Constitution promises its citizens freedom of speech and press, the CCP uses vague claims regarding the protection of government secrets to legitimize its oppressive practices. In other words, Chinese citizens can say what they want as long as the government approves of what they say.

Like a page out of Orwell's *Nineteen Eighty-Four*, China's most powerful enforcement division is the Communist Party's Central Propaganda Department (CPD). According to one report, the government rewrote an article in a popular magazine, altering it from a piece that called for political change to one that exalted the CCP. In 2009, activist Liu Xiaobo issued pleas for democracy and human rights in China. For this, he was sentenced to 11 years in prison, marking the fourth time he was incarcerated. Notably, he won the Nobel Peace Prize for his work.[18]

THE WEST

It is easy for us to overlook what is happening in China because we don't consider it a threat to our freedom in America. But what about a country closer to home, like Canada? Reporters Without Borders revealed that freedom of speech and the press has plummeted in Canada, dropping ten spots on RWB's international rankings. In 2017, the country received failing marks because of its surveillance of journalists and persecution of whistleblowers.[19] One journalist, Justin Brake, reportedly faced up to ten years in prison for covering a protest for *The Independent* in 2016.[20] As of 2022, the government is advancing several pieces of legislation designed to target free speech.[21]

And Canadian news is becoming increasingly more government-controlled, like China. Back in 1936, Canada created the Canadian Broadcasting Corporation (CBC). It is a taxpayer-funded communications corporation, much like America's PBS. But, unlike America, nearly every news organization in Canada is funded by the Canadian government. There are fewer than a handful of independent news outlets. The CBC favors specific types of messaging and has all but abandoned journalistic independence. The vast majority of Canadians get their news from CBC.[22]

During the COVID pandemic, Prime Minister Justin Trudeau said unvaccinated Canadians were people who "often don't believe in science," labeling them as "misogynist" and "racist." He asked if those people should be "tolerated by society." Trudeau also blamed the lockdowns and health-care worker shortages on unvaccinated individuals. Days later, the country announced mandatory vaccinations, and virtually none of the news outlets revealed that, at the time, there were more vaccinated people in hospitals than unvaccinated.[23]

If you're reading this in the US, you should immediately recognize this kind of demonization because many Americans who were reluctant about the COVID vaccine were talked about this way by governors in the US and even by President Joe Biden. For a government to demonize large groups of people is dangerous, and it can lead to widespread persecution.

Reports reveal that the editors at CBC have been pushing divisive news stories about race and will not allow any debate on issues like vaccination and housing costs. In 2019, the news organization was caught lying when it stated that 40 percent of Canadians experienced racism at work, but the poll actually said 8 percent. In the spirit of controlling language, CBC encouraged reporters to use the phrase "climate crisis" instead of "climate change" to invoke fear in the public.[24]

This is reminiscent of what I found during the Breonna Taylor case. The facts of her shooting were sad enough. Why did the media feel the need to spread lies about her being shot in her sleep? Because it aroused more anger from the public.

Like the dystopian government in *Nineteen Eighty-Four*, CBC has actually created documentaries that rewrite history. One World War 2 documentary depicted the Allied powers' bombing of Germany as genocide (similarly, Israel has recently been wrongly accused by governments and the media of genocide). When World War 2 veterans created a documentary countering that narrative about the bombings, CBC would not air it. America's PBS aired it instead.[25]

Like China, Canada promises its citizens freedom of speech and press.[26] Still, Trudeau's regime proposed bills in early 2022 designed to tighten its controls on media content. The bills would allow the government to ban what it claimed to be "hate speech" on the internet in Canada, penalize violators with fines, and expand the country's power to monitor content.[27]

But nothing compares to the onslaught of derogatory coverage of religious citizens in Canada, which has already turned into legal persecution.[28] One bill, which passed the National Assembly of Quebec, prohibits government workers from wearing religious clothing or symbols at work.[29] And Canada denied a Christian law school accreditation because it requires all its students to adhere to its statement of faith and code of conduct. Canada said the school's beliefs were in direct contradiction to the nation's wholehearted embrace of unbiblical practices relating to sexual orientation and gender identity. In an article titled "Canada Attacks Religious Freedom," Bob Kuhn from the *Wall Street Journal* wrote,

> The Law Society of Upper Canada, the nation's oldest and largest, told the high court in Ottawa during oral arguments on Nov. 30, 2017, that accrediting any "distinctly religious" organization would violate the Canadian Charter, which is similar to the U.S. Bill of Rights. It added that when the government licenses a private organization it adopts all its policies as its own. If these arguments had been accepted, they would have spelled the end of Canada's nonprofit sector. In their zeal to root out the supposed bigotry of traditional religious believers, these lawyers were prepared to dynamite Canada's entire civil society. Thankfully, the court passed over some of our opponents' more extreme arguments. Instead, on June 15, it ruled that making Trinity's faith-based community standards mandatory could harm the dignity of members of the LGBT community who attend Trinity. The majority of the court concluded

that this potential dignitary harm to future LGBT law students was "concrete," while the infringement on Trinity's religious liberty from refusing to accredit its qualified law program was "minimal."[30]

And the legal threats to Christians don't end in civil court. During the COVID pandemic, Canadian Pastor Artur Pawlowski was jailed repeatedly for holding worship services and preaching against government mandates. Several pastors and religious leaders were jailed during that time.[31]

Even worse, the country now imposes jail time for people who speak against immoral sexual practices. As reported by the *Washington Times*, "Canada's recently unanimously passed law, C-4, prevents its citizens from spreading Biblical views on marriage and sexuality. Canadian parents, faith leaders, and citizens who hold traditional views of marriage and sexuality will now face up to 5 years of jail time for providing spiritual guidance to those seeking counseling."[32]

CONTROLLING THE NARRATIVE

You can already see where this is going. Once we analyze Canada's demonization of Christians and others who speak against the government's preferred messages, we can see that America is on the fast track to ideological tyranny.

Much of this starts with the way the West has adopted language that influences how people think about certain topics. In *Nineteen Eighty-Four*, Orwell talks about Newspeak, which limits language to discourage people from speaking or thinking thoughts that violate the government's ideology. The word *thoughtcrime* was used to describe any thought a person had that opposed the government. The idea that language can be used to influence a person's thoughts is called linguistic relativity.[33] Let's look at a few examples of this in American culture.

In a notable exchange that took place during a Senate Judiciary Committee hearing, Senator Josh Hawley asked a UC Berkeley law professor what she meant when she spoke about "people with the capacity for pregnancy."[34] When he asked her whether she was referring to women, she asked whether he was "denying that trans people exist." Notice the deflection here. She didn't answer his question. Instead, she went in a different direction—one designed to change the entire foundation of his point, which is *the* point when it comes to the transgender debate. Confirming that only women can get pregnant does not deny anyone's mental state. But framing the argument this way limits the ability to debate the issue from a factual and biological perspective.

This issue in particular cannot be debated apart from using the correct language. Accepting the baseless assertion that a man is a woman because he claims to be one leads to all sorts of diabolical assumptions about the nature of human beings. We know that God has made sexual identity fixed, and His standards do not change based on someone's feelings. We cannot use language or words that have been redefined to force us to adopt a worldly framework. It is wrong for people to deny what is factually and biologically true about themselves. We are who God says we are.

Florida's Parental Rights in Education bill—which was passed in 2022—prohibits instruction on sexual orientation or gender identity from kindergarten through the third grade. Activists smeared it as the "Don't say gay" bill. Despite the fact the bill is designed to prevent children from being exposed to sexually explicit content at a young age, the mainstream media persisted in making it about censoring speech. But despite the attempted demonization of the law, a poll earlier this year by Public Opinion Strategies revealed that 61 percent of people supported it, including 55 percent of Democrats. Only 26 percent of people opposed it.[35] This is a clear example of the mainstream media creating a false narrative in an attempt to deceive people.

Even accepting the common framing that sexual preferences or gender dysphoria are identities is a tool designed to get the public to accept that renouncing the behaviors is akin to attacking the person. It is a ploy to convince the public that defining certain behavioral practices as immoral is synonymous with invidious discrimination. But it is not. Remember the bridge the world is trying to build between racial supremacy and those who advocate for sexual morality? We must resist this deception whenever it presents itself.

Doing this means being willing to speak up even when we are surrounded by people who do not agree with us. And the broader our platform, the more responsibility we have to speak. The problem is that even when we know something is wrong, we are afraid to speak our convictions. We refrain from saying anything because we don't want people to disagree with us.

In a recent national poll commissioned by Times Opinion and Siena College, only 34 percent of Americans said they believed that all Americans enjoyed freedom of speech completely. The poll found that 84 percent of adults said it is a "very serious" or "somewhat serious" problem that some Americans do not speak freely in everyday situations because they fear retaliation or harsh criticism.[36]

More than that, many Americans have adopted the narrative that "hate speech" should be censored even though it is constitutionally protected. However, as we'll see in a moment, statistics demonstrate why it is necessary for hate speech to be legally protected. People vary in their opinions about what constitutes hate speech—it's a largely subjective issue. This makes it impossible to create an objective framework for identifying hate speech.

For example, about 59 percent of Americans think people should be allowed to share unpopular opinions, even if some find those ideas offensive. But 40 percent think that the government should enforce hate speech mandates in public. What people don't realize is that while it might be easy to identify hate speech when it comes in the form of a racial slur, it is not that simple when it comes to ideologically charged issues. Consider these statistics, which demonstrate how the "degree of offense" can vary depending on whether someone is a Democrat or a Republican:

- 51 percent of those who are strongly liberal say it's "morally acceptable" to punch Nazis.

- 53 percent of Republicans favor stripping US citizenship from people who burn the American flag.

- 51 percent of Democrats support a law that requires Americans to use transgender people's preferred gender pronouns.

- 47 percent of Republicans favor bans on building new mosques.

- 58 percent of Democrats say employers should punish employees for offensive Facebook posts.

- 65 percent of Republicans say NFL players should be fired if they refuse to stand for the national anthem.[37]

In *The Origins of Totalitarianism*, Hannah Arendt reveals that propaganda and the willingness to believe "useful lies" prepares the ground for tyranny. She further notes that disdain for others is the primary reason that people willingly exchange the truth for lies.[38] What this means in this context is that we are more likely to want free speech for ourselves but not for those we despise, and we are more likely to tolerate hateful speech when it is directed at our perceived enemies.

But the culture is doing its job. It is convincing the next generation—through educational institutions and the media—that hate speech mandates are a good thing. In a Pew Research Center survey, an astounding 64 percent of young people ages 13 to 17 said that free speech is not as important as people feeling safe and welcome online. Nearly half (47 percent) of adults over 18 said that free speech is more important than protecting people's feelings online.[39]

It is important to note here that there is a fine line between freedom and tyranny. Censoring offensive speech might seem like the more compassionate thing to do, but the problem is that there is no way to draw the line between what is offensive and what is necessary opposition. History is unanimous in its witness that once we allow the government to censor speech it doesn't like, we will no longer possess freedom of speech. And all independent, objective voices in the press will become extinct, as is true in China and increasingly in Canada.

Benito Mussolini defined totalitarianism as follows: "Everything within the state, nothing outside the state, nothing against the state."[40] Ultimately, when the government wants to control you, it must ensure that everything you say is aligned with its will.

TAKE ADVANTAGE OF THE CROWD

In Matthew 5, when Jesus saw that a crowd had assembled, He went up a mountainside and began to teach (verse 1). He gave what many consider to be the greatest speech of all time: the Sermon on the Mount. The most notable detail in this passage, for our purposes in this chapter, is that Jesus took advantage of the opportunity to spread the gospel to a large crowd of people.

The Bible tells us repeatedly how powerful our words are. They can shape lives (James 3:1-18). Scripture explicitly and implicitly informs us that our words can persuade others and draw them into the kingdom of God (Proverbs 16:23 ESV: "The heart of the wise makes his speech judicious and adds persuasiveness to his lips"). We are told that we can overcome Satan by the blood of the lamb and by the word of our testimony (Revelation 12:11). Consider how rapidly the gospel spread from only a few disciples. Our words are powerful tools that can influence the culture for Christ.

For this reason, we must take advantage of our spheres of influence and share God's truth and love with as many people as possible. Social media can be useful in this regard. It's possible to share our testimony with only a few people or many—even millions—in a matter of moments.

But the power of words is not limited to believers. Secular people and institutions can use words to achieve their purposes. Oftentimes, the microphone is held by those who do not know God. The media has enormous control over what is communicated and what isn't, and uses this power to deceive many, including believers. While Christians can use different forms of media to share truth with a wide range of people, we must also be vigilant about what we read and hear. Through the media, we are susceptible to Satan's cunning rhetoric, spread in the form of lies and deceptions.

Because of the vast network Satan has at his disposal through the media, people are likely to hear his lies more than they hear God's truth. Repetition is powerful, which is the reason that, over time, Christians can end up losing their moral convictions. The facts we explored earlier about the decline of sexual morality are the result of an unending stream of pornographic images that have bombarded people for decades on TV and the internet. Think, for example, about how taboo it once was for people to live together before they were married, or for a woman to be pregnant out of wedlock. The media has slowly desensitized society to these behaviors so that they are now considered ordinary and accepted, as opposed to immoral.

This is why Christians must become guarded and discerning about what they watch—to ensure their consciences do not become seared to the point of lacking sensitivity. Satan wants to sear our consciences. He knows that the more we see and hear that something is right even when it is wrong, the more we will accept it. This is why we must be so careful.

Orwell makes this point in *Nineteen Eighty-Four*: "We do not destroy the heretic because he resists us...We convert him, we capture his inner mind, we reshape him."[41] While some cultures took a more direct approach to forcefully subjugating their population, the most sophisticated tyrannical regimes instead change the public's mind so that its citizens willingly accept the new establishment.

This is much easier than fighting resistance. For this reason, some of the countries we've already studied used mass media to control the people.

The examples we've examined reveal the dangerous path we are on in America. As with the tyrannical regimes of old, more and more, the government in America is choosing its preferred ideologies, demonizing those who oppose them, controlling words and language so that people cannot articulate opposition, and slowly coercing people to tolerate persecution and the extermination of the undesirables.

Every Christian has a sphere of influence, and we must commit to using ours to spread truth. Right now, nearly three out of every four adults use social media.[42] This means almost every Christian has established an audience, no matter how small, to which they can speak about the truth of the gospel. If we all use our influence for what is right and good, we could counter many of the false narratives that dominate the mainstream media.

> *Every Christian has a sphere of influence, and we must commit to using ours to spread truth.*

Remember also that social media is designed to induce conflict between people. According to a report from the *Wall Street Journal*, Facebook conducted internal research in 2018 that demonstrated that its "algorithms exploit the human brain's attraction to divisiveness."[43] This means we must resist the urge to argue and be in conflict, and instead, seek to spread truth with compassion.

There are times when people will attack you for your beliefs, but you don't have to participate in their ire.

What about the fact that social media allows us to shield ourselves from competing views and ideas? It's possible for us to create walls around ourselves and to ostracize the people whom we disagree with. This is equally as problematic as engaging in constant conflict. We must be able to see people as being in the image of God and not demonize them because of their beliefs. We must find this balance when we use social media.

Finding that balance is key because Christians need to get out on that mount and proclaim God's good news. Contrary to what believers often assume, many people are willing to engage with Christian content even though they don't follow Christ. According to Lifeway Research studies, the COVID pandemic expanded the reach of online church services. Almost half of all Americans say they watched at least one service during the pandemic, including 15 percent who said they normally do not attend in person. Overall, few Americans say they consume Christian-based media, but most have at least occasionally watched Christian TV or read a Christian book. Half of all Americans said they watched Christian content in the past year.[44] We should take advantage of this openness and ensure that we make content aimed at unbelievers as well as believers.

We must also be alert to the fact that progressive views, which are contrary to biblical views, are widespread in the media. This means the public is constantly being bombarded with ideas intended to change the way they think and to convince them to embrace lies. Lies that were once widely rejected have become the norm. Unfortunately, many Christians are deceived by what they hear, and as a result, they abandon biblical doctrine. We must remain prayerful and constant in God's Word to avoid this.

> With them indeed is fulfilled the prophecy of Isaiah which says: "You shall indeed hear but never understand, and you shall indeed see but never perceive. For this people's heart has grown dull, and their ears are heavy of hearing, and their eyes they have closed, lest they should perceive with their eyes and hear with their ears, and understand with their heart, and turn to me to heal them." But blessed are your eyes for they see, and your ears, for they hear (Matthew 13:14-16 NRSV).

Even though Christians can and should use the media to create Christian music, entertainment, news, and social media content, remember, the media is still controlled by the world. It is part of Satan's territory, so we should always expect to be the underdog in that realm. It's as if we are living as exiles in Babylon. We live in the tension between seeking to make good use of the media yet never succumbing to its many lures designed to pull us away from God and believe the world's lies. Let's use the power of our tongues to influence the world for the kingdom of God. We are to be salt and light in this culture in all that we do and say.

PART 4

CAN GOD
SEND YOU?

CHAPTER 11

TAKE THE STAND

Spiritual freedom is found in God alone. A relationship with Jesus Christ provides us with access to God's wisdom, protection, and guidance, which opens the door to a life of liberty and purpose. Without Him, we are slaves to our flesh, bowing to our internal, insatiable desires, motived and driven by the tyrant within us.

Satan is the ruler of this world, and his predominant desire is to remove God's influence from the lives of people everywhere. He seeks to run the world and do away with God's commandments and standards. Everything Satan does is meant to dethrone God as ruler.

And much like he did with Adam and Eve, Satan arouses the tyrannical desire that exists within all of us to be like God and rule our lives without Him.

We must be united in our commitment to yielding to God's rule over the church. We must constantly remind ourselves that we belong to Him, and nothing should deter us from pledging our allegiance to His throne. We are kingdom citizens on earth, ambassadors of heaven, sent to be imitators of Christ for the world. We are proof of His power, His truth, and His love.

Thus, as we seek to walk with Him individually, we must allow Him to use us to impact the broader society, spreading His truth to everyone within our spheres of influence. Knowing God and making Him known to others are our primary missions. We should boldly and intentionally embody Him in our everyday lives.

At the same time, we should strive to live rightly and honorably in a society that allows us to live out God's mission for our lives. We should never let the government or any leader to circumvent our divine mission. Any ruling agency that exercises such authority over us is engaging in tyranny—it is making government supreme over God, which is what Satan desires. For this reason, we as Christians must be educated about how governments establish tyrannical rule, so that we can be vigilant in protecting our divine callings and God's kingdom agenda.

We must be God's watchmen, for the church and our own hearts. As we have seen through our study of tyranny throughout history, tyranny begins by destroying the conscience of society. A godless ruler must attack those who will not obey him above all else. Because believers will never bow to edicts that remove God's place of authority in their lives, they must be eradicated.

Because we dwell on this earth, all believers are involved in politics in some way. It is through politics that citizens engage with their government. We will always be involved in this intractable conflict as long as we are here—that is, if we are truly advancing God's kingdom agenda. People like David, Peter, Paul, Esther, Daniel, Joseph, and even Jesus, just to name a few, are your biblical reminders that this intersection between Christianity and government is unavoidable.

The church must accept this responsibility. This requires us to be able to recognize unjust governmental actions. And the church should teach each member how to maintain their own conscience and protect themselves from deception. We should also be maintaining our reverence for God, which includes accepting who He is and who He says we are. As Christians, we must know and accept that our identity is bound in what God says, and not in what we believe or what other people think about us.

As Christians, we must know and accept that our identity is bound in what God says, and not in what we believe or what other people think about us.

We must also remember that everyone is made in the image of God. We should respect the imago Dei within everyone and resist the urge to exercise supremacist behaviors over others. Those in the church should be the loudest protestors against the unjust treatment of people in our society.

Individually, all Christians should walk with God to fulfill His mission for their life. In the course of knowing God and making Him known, we will be assigned to various roles through which God can accomplish His kingdom agenda.

In this book, we reviewed three areas where I see a great need for Christian influence. But there are more areas, and each believer should seek God's guidance as they yield their passions and skills to His use. My experiences as a teacher and a constitutional lawyer have given me insight into the justice system, education, and media. And I would encourage believers to use their giftedness and past experiences to fulfill God's kingdom agenda on whatever path God places you.

Because all of us do interact with the justice system, education, and the media at various points of our lives, my hope is that you've found this book helpful toward giving you ideas for having a greater influence on others.

The way a society administers justice is key to ensuring that the government stays within its proper bounds of power. The American justice system should protect its citizens from government overreach and administer appropriate punishment to people who break the laws. And it should maintain people's freedoms.

Education is vital to a free society. People who are ignorant are easily controlled. We should actively advocate for a liberated education for all—one that provides students with the ability to obtain moral, social, and academically rigorous instruction.

Communication includes the news, entertainment, and social media. Not only should Christians seek to influence these areas so they can proclaim God's truth to the culture, they should also recognize when these mediums are communicating lies. This will require you to educate yourself on relevant issues and not assume that the world is always providing accurate information. Every believer should protect their mind from deception by filtering, through the Word of God, every bit of information they read and hear.

A LIFE OF INFLUENCE

There are many reasons the church is losing its influence in secular society. We've explored a few of them. We are in a crucial time when the church needs to reclaim its position as the moral compass of the culture. We are to set ourselves on a hill and be a beacon that shines God's light, and to be unapologetically devoted to God's standards (Matthew 5:14).

We are in a crucial time when the church needs to reclaim its position as the moral compass of the culture.

We also need to remember that Satan often masquerades as an angel of light. This alerts us to the fact there are people who will claim to be Christians yet, in reality, they defame the name of Jesus. For example, there are churches and pastors who celebrate evil practices like abortion and claim that Jesus is prochoice. This is clearly error, and all believers should recognize it as such.

It is also possible for believers to be deceived. As we've seen in some of the examples throughout this book, Christians can be deceived to advocate for the kingdom of darkness rather than God's kingdom. But this is a separate issue than that of Satan masquerading as a messenger of light. It may be difficult for us to spot such deceptions. That's why we have to be very careful about who we trust.

When it comes to true believers who happen to be deceived and you know them well enough to realize they are in fact Christians, your goal should be to help them see truth. One mistake we often make in the church is to publicly criticize a Christian who strays or falls but fail to pursue them and bring them back to truth.

James 5:19-20 tells us that anyone who turns a sinner from the error of his ways will save that sinner from death and cover over a multitude of sins. Such an act of love will benefit both the sinner and the believer who seeks to deliver the wandering brother or sister. The verse promises that such an act covers a multitude of sins for both parties. It would behoove every believer to remember this, and the church should teach its members to reach out to each other when we stumble.

We are responsible for one another, and the church should be a soft place to land for every believer and for people in the world who are hurting. This doesn't mean that we sacrifice truth for a false perception of compassion by compromising God's standards to appease others. It means that we make sure everyone knows that God loves them and welcomes them into His kingdom. While no one will come to Him perfect, nor be perfect while here on earth, it is imperative that our goal is to let God conform us to His Son's image. We must let Him mold us and dominate the flesh inside of us.

A WALL OF SEPARATION
BETWEEN CHURCH AND SATAN

The culture despises Christians because they illuminate the culture's separation from God. We are a painful reminder that the culture's desires are insatiable and nothing will ever fulfill people's inner longings but God. The world hates believers because it hates Jesus Christ.

A culture without God produces people with depraved minds. They are unable to think rationally, and they embrace and engage

in all kinds of wicked behaviors as a result. When people abandon God, He will abandon them and give them a glimpse of what
life is like without Him (Romans 1:28-31). He will give them over
to their desires. He will squelch the conviction within them, and
they will be slaves to their worldly longings. People will become
incapable of rational thinking and their emotions will be their
god. And the culture will do everything it can to persuade, pressure, and penalize Christians to make them join its side.

Our ability to resist the culture's demands will determine the
power of our divine influence. The more we give in, the more our
influence will diminish; the more we resist, the more powerful
we will be in the culture. Our impact will be measured by how
closely we are aligned with God's agenda. Our actions should be
the proverbial wall that separates the church from the world and
from Satan and his agenda.

*Our ability to resist the culture's demands will
determine the power of our divine influence.*

MASTER YOUR DEFENSE

As a lawyer, my job is to know the law and use it to defend my clients. I can't be an effective advocate for my clients without understanding the law and believing in the justice system. Likewise, an
effective witness for Christ must be a student of the Bible. But even
more, anyone who wants to publicly advocate for God's truth in
the culture must be a committed Christian apologist. That means

you not only know and believe the gospel, but you can defend it. You should "[a]lways be ready to make your defense to anyone who demands from you an accounting for the hope that is in you, yet do it with gentleness and respect" (1 Peter 3:15-16).

Even though God puts emphasis on your faith, He still makes a persuasive case about why you can trust Him. You should take time to study the evidence to support the gospel and use it to reignite your walk and improve your evangelism. Apologetics makes us more committed to our faith because we know that our beliefs are built on a firm foundation.

Much like we should take the time to evaluate any worldview we embrace, we should know the evidence to support Christianity. Thankfully, that evidence is worth learning and telling. There is compelling evidence that the disciples' claims about Jesus are credible and that the Bible is historically accurate. You should especially know the evidence to support the event that is the foundation for our belief system: the resurrection (1 Corinthians 15:16-19).

There's no question that the best direct evidence of Christianity are the eyewitness testimonies in the gospels. In *The Case for Christ*, Lee Strobel said, "[T]he manuscript evidence for the New Testament was overwhelming when juxtaposed against other revered writings of antiquity—works that modern scholars have absolutely no reluctance treating as authentic."[1] Compared to other ancient works, historians are confident that the Gospels were passed down accurately.[2] The earliest piece of papyrus is from the Nile Delta in Egypt. The piece is from the book of John and dates back to AD 100 to 150, close to the time when Jesus walked the earth. Former director of the British Museum and author of *The Palaeography of Greek Papyri* said that "in no other case is the interval of time between the composition of the book and the date of the earliest manuscripts so short as in that of the New Testament."[3]

As for Jesus' resurrection, no credible objections about the event exist during that period.[4] There is conclusive medical evidence that Jesus died on the cross from asphyxia and blood loss. By all accounts, Jesus' tomb was empty. Most compelling are Jesus' postresurrection appearances. Jesus appeared to more than 500 people after His public death. People not only saw Him, but they interacted with Him. Jesus notably appeared to Mary Magdalene. Then He appeared to the apostle Peter and ten other apostles, and the witnesses of His ascension.[5]

But the most powerful evidence for the gospel are our personal conversions because we are living examples of how Jesus transforms lives. Because He has revealed Himself to us, we are supposed to tell people about what we know. Consider the dramatic conversion of the apostle Paul.

Paul despised Christians so much that he slaughtered them. Then one day on the road to Damascus, Christ appeared to Paul and called him to become a follower. Paul went on to become a Christian who would risk his life to tell others about the gospel. His conversion was so dramatic that it demonstrated Jesus' transformative power to everyone who encountered Paul.

We stand on unshakable truth; we should always be proud to be Jesus' witnesses to the world.

The truth is timeless, and it will never become outdated or irrelevant. That's the reason our own conversions can be as influential as Paul's. We stand on unshakable truth; we should always be proud to be Jesus' witnesses to the world. We should be fearless advocates for the gospel no matter the cost. That's the uncommon courage you and I are called to.

NOTES

CHAPTER 1: CHRISTIANITY AND THE CONSTITUTION

1. John Eidsmoe, *Christianity and the Constitution: The Faith of the Founding Fathers* (Grand Rapids, MI: Baker, 1987), 341.

2. Ibid.

3. Ibid.

4. Ibid., 20.

5. Ibid., 73.

6. Ibid.

7. Ibid., 62.

8. Ibid., 11.

9. Ibid., 11, 21.

10. Ibid., 11.

11. Ibid., 73.

12. Ibid., 367.

13. Ibid., 366.

14. Ibid., 267.

15. James Madison, *The Federalist No. 51, The Federalist Papers*, ed. Clinton Rossier (New York: Mentor Books, 1961), 322.

16. Eidsmoe, *Christianity and the Constitution*, 347.

17. Ibid.

18. Dan Currell & Elle Rogers, "The Invisible American Founding" *National Affairs*, Winter 2024, https://www.nationalaffairs.com/publications/detail/the-invisible-american-founding.

CHAPTER 2: THE ROADMAP TO TYRANNY

1. Hannah Arendt, *The Origins of Totalitarianism* (New York: Houghton Mifflin Harcourt, 1951), 325.

2. *Five Steps to Tyranny*, directed by Elizabeth McIntyre, *BBC*, 2001.

3. Rod Dreher, *Live Not by Lies* (New York: Sentinel, 2020), 31.

4. Ibid.

5. *Five Steps to Tyranny*.

6. George Orwell, *Nineteen Eighty-Four* (New York: Signet Classic, 1950), Part II, Chapter IX.

7. Dreher, *Live Not by Lies,* 35.

8. Kenneth Roth, "China e Tibete," *Human Rights Watch*, October 5, 2023, https://www.hrw.org/pt/asia/china-e-tibete#.

9. "Custom Report Excerpts: China, Hong Kong, Macau, Tibet," *US Department of State*, https://www.state.gov/report/custom/53bdb8b7f1/.

10. Ibid.

11. Ibid.

12. Annie Boyajian, "Leveraging Targeted Sanctions in Defense of Religious Freedom," *Freedom House*, November 11, 2021, https://freedomhouse.org/article/leveraging-targeted-sanctions-defense-religious-freedom.

13. Patrick Farrell, "China's 'Social Credit' Monitoring: Big Brother's Frightening New Tool for Repression," *The Heritage Foundation*, November 4, 2018, https://www.heritage.org/international-economies/commentary/chinas-social-credit-monitoring-big-brothers-frightening-new; Kaite Canales, "China's 'social credit' system ranks citizens and punishes them with throttled internet speeds and flight bans if the Communist Party deems them untrustworthy," *Business Insider*, December 24, 2021, https://www.businessinsider.com/china-social-credit-system-punishments-and-rewards-explained-2018-4.

14. Thomas Carothers and Andrew O'Donohue, *Democracies Divided: The Global Challenge of Political Polarization* (Washington, DC: Brookings Institution Press, 2019), i–iv, http://www.jstor.org/stable/10.7864/j.ctvbd8j2p.1.

15. Rod Dreher, *Live Not by Lies,* 7.

16. Ibid., 10.

17. Tim Radford, "The Blame Game," *The Guardian*, December 18, 2000, https://www.theguardian.com/media/2000/dec/19/tvandradio.television1.

CHAPTER 3: A CONSCIENCE CONTRARY TO TYRANNY

1. "The Obsolete Man," *The Twilight Zone*, season 2, episode 29, directed by Elliot Silverstein, June 2, 1961, on CBS.

2. "The Obsolete Man," *The Twilight Zone.*

3. "The Obsolete Man," *The Twilight Zone.*

4. Marion Smith, "Communism and Religion Can't Coexist," *The Wall Street Journal*, August 29, 2019, https://www.wsj.com/articles/communism-and-religion-cant-coexist-11567120938 (accessed Aug. 23, 2021).

5. Giles Fraser, "Why the Soviet attempt to stamp out religion failed," *The Guardian*, October 26, 2017, https://www.theguardian.com/commentisfree/belief/2017/oct/26/why-the-soviet-attempt-to-stamp-out-religion-failed.

6. Ibid.

7. "Revelations from the Russian Archives: Internal Workings of the Soviet Union," *Library of Congress*, https://www.loc.gov/exhibits/archives/intn.html.

8. Ibid.

9. Smith, "Communism and Religion Can't Coexist."

10. Ibid.

11. Joe Starkey, "Word for Word/The Case Against the Nazis; How Hitler's Forces Planned to Destroy German Christianity," *New York Times*, January 13, 2002, Section 4, Page 7.

12. Ibid.

13. Ibid.

14. Ibid.

15. Ibid.

16. Ibid.

17. Adolf Hitler, speech in Passau, October 27, 1928.

18. Ian Kershaw, *Hitler: A Biography* (London: W.W. Norton, 2008), 381-82.

19. Fred Taylor, trans., *The Goebbels Diaries 1939-41* (London: Hamish Hamilton Ltd, 1982), 76.

20. Otto Strasser, *Hitler and I* (Boston, MA: Houghton Mifflin Company, 1940), 93.

21. *Third Reich: The Rise*, directed by Seth Skundrick, History Channel, 2010, TV mini-series.

22. Samuel Koehne, "Hitler's faith: The debate over Nazism and religion," *ABC News*, April 17, 2020, https://www.abc.net.au/religion/hitlers-faith-the-debate-over-nazism-and-religion/10100614.

23. William L. Shirer, *The Rise and Fall of the Third Reich: A History of Nazi Germany* (New York: Simon and Schuster, 2011), 240.

24. Franklin D. Roosevelt, "Address for Navy and Total Defense Day" (October 27, 1941) at Gerhard Peters and John T. Woolley, *The American Presidency Project,* https://www.presidency.ucsb.edu/node/210207.

25. Alan Bullock, *Hitler: A Study in Tyranny* (New York: Harper, 1991), 2, 18.

26. United States Holocaust Memorial Museum, "The German Churches and the Nazi State," *Holocaust Encyclopedia*, https://encyclopedia.ushmm.org/content/en/article/the-german-churches-and-the-nazi-state.

27. Ibid.

28. Smith, "Communism and Religion Can't Coexist."

29. Azeem Ibrahim, "The Chinese Communist Party Is Scared of Christianity," *Foreign Policy*, July 1, 2021, https://foreignpolicy.com/2021/07/01/chinese-communist-party-scared-of-christianity-religion/; Walter Russell Mead, "Beijing's Collision with Christians," *The Wall Street Journal*, December 21, 2020, https://www.wsj.com/articles/beijings-collision-with-christians-11608593160.

30. Ibid.

31. Ibrahim, "The Chinese Communist Party Is Scared of Christianity;" Mead, "Beijing's Collision with Christians."

32. Mead, "Beijing's Collision with Christians."

33. Smith, "Communism and Religion Can't Coexist."

34. Ibrahim, "The Chinese Communist Party Is Scared of Christianity."

35. Cameron Hilditch, "China's Communist Christ," *National Review*, October 1, 2020, https://www.nationalreview.com/2020/10/chinas-communist-christ/.

36. Ibid.

37. Rod Dreher, *Live Not by Lies* (New York: Sentinel, 2020), 85.

38. 1 Annals of Congress 730, August 15, 1789.

39. See, for example: Bishop O.C. Allen III and Rabbi Michael Rothbaum, "Stop peddling LGBTQ discrimination in name of religion," *Atlanta Journal-Constitution*, February 24, 2024, https://www.ajc.com/opinion/stop-peddling-lgbtq-discrimination-in-name-of-rel igion/3FCT3MSS65FHDEPBHU2GQZAVTQ/; Tisa Wenger, "Discriminating in the name of religion? Segregationists and slaveholders did it, too," *The Washington Post*, December 5, 2017, https://www.washingtonpost.com/news/made-by-history/wp/2017/12/05/discriminating-in-the-name-of-religion-segregationists-and-slaveholders-did-it-too/.

40. "Chairman Nadler's Statement for the Markup of H.R. 5, the Equality Act," https://nadler.house.gov/news/documentsingle.aspx?DocumentID=393904.

41. *Obergefell v. Hodges*, 576 U.S. 644, 741 (2015).

42. Thomas Jefferson, "Jefferson's Letter to the Danbury Baptists" (Jan. 1, 1802), *Library of Congress*, June 1998, https://www.loc.gov/loc/lcib/9806/danpre.html.

43. *American Legion v. American Humanist Association*, 139 S. Ct. 2067 (2019).

44. *Kennedy v. Bremerton School District*, 142 S. Ct. 2407 (2022).

45. *Trinity Lutheran Church of Columbia, Inc. v. Comer*, 137 S. Ct. 2012 (2017); *Espinoza v. Montana Dep't of Revenue*, 140 S. Ct. 2246 (2020); *Carson v. Makin*, 142 S. Ct. 1987 (2022).

46. Address by Justice Samuel Alito, Federalist Society National Lawyers Convention, November 12, 2020, https://www.youtube.com/watch?v=VMnukCVIZWQ.

47. Jeffrey M. Jones, "U.S. Church Membership Falls Below Majority for the First Time," *Gallup*, March 29, 2021, https://news.gallup.com/poll/341963/church-membership-falls-below-majority-first-time.aspx.

48. *On Fire Christian Ctr., Inc. v. Fischer*, 453 F. Supp. 3d 901, 905 (W.D. Ky. 2020).

49. *The Diocese of Brooklyn v. Cuomo*, 141 S. Ct. 63 (2020).

50. Mead, "Beijing's Collision with Christians."

51. Ibid.

CHAPTER 4: FEAR GOD

1. Dreher, *Live Not by Lies* (New York: Sentinel, 2020) xiii, footnote 2.

2. Ibid., 28.

3. Tony Evans, *Kingdom Politics* (Nashville, TN: Lifeway, 2023), 2.

4. Ibid.

5. Dreher, *Live Not by Lies*, 12.

6. Sophie Hayssen, "What Are the Comstock Laws? Here's How They Influenced Sex Ed Debates," *Teen Vogue*, February 15, 2022, https://www.teenvogue.com/story/what-are-comstock-laws.

7. Geoffrey Stone, "'Sex and the Constitution': Margaret Sanger and the birth of the birth control movement," *The Washington Post*, March 24, 2017, https://www.washingtonpost.com/news/volokh-conspiracy/wp/2017/03/24/sex-and-the-constitution-margaret-sanger-and-the-birth-of-the-birth-control-movement/.

8. Terry Gross, "How An Anti-Vice Crusader Sabotaged The Early Birth Control Movement," *NPR*, July 7, 2021, https://www.npr.org/2021/07/07/1013592570/how-an-anti-vice-crusader-sabotaged-the-early-birth-control-movement.

9. Ibid.

10. "How the Sexual Revolution Changed American Culture," *Proven Men*, August 19, 2016, https://www.provenmen.org/sexual-revolution-changed-american-culture/.

11. Scott Yenor, "The Deregulation of Pornography," *Heritage Foundation*, May 19, 2020, https://www.heritage.org/marriage-and-family/report/postmortem-the-sexual-revolution-what-deregulation-pornography-has.

12. Ibid.

13. David Lowenthal, *No Liberty for License: The Forgotten Logic of the First Amendment* (Dallas, TX: Spence Publishing, 1997), 87-107, 136-150. Harry M. Clor, *Obscenity and Public Morality: Censorship in a Liberal Society* (Chicago: University of Chicago, 1969), 14-87. ("The most prominent Supreme Court cases in effect integrating the sexual revolution into the Constitution include *Roth v. United States*, 354 U.S. 476 [1957], making regulation of obscenity and pornography difficult; *Griswold v. Connecticut* 381 U.S. 479 [1965], invalidating state laws on contraception on the grounds of the "right to privacy"; and especially *Lawrence v. Texas*, 539 U.S. 558 [2003], invalidating state laws outlawing sodomy, and *Obergefell v. Hodges* 576 U.S. 644 [2015], requiring that states recognize same-sex marriage.")

14. Ibid.

15. Scott Yenor, "The Deregulation of Pornography."

16. Ibid.

17. Emma Waters, "Crushing Society's Building Block," *Heritage Foundation*, September 30, 2022, https://www.heritage.org/marriage-and-family/commentary/crushing-societys-building-block.

18. Ibid.

19. Ibid.

20. *Ginzburg v. United States*, 383 U.S. 463, 489-490 (1966).

21. Emma Waters, "Crushing Society's Building Block," citing Paul Robinson, *The Modernization of Sex: Havelock Ellis, Alfred Kinsey, William Masters and Virginia Johnson* (New York: Harper & Row, 1976), 55-56.

22. Emma Waters, "Crushing Society's Building Block," citing Alfred C. Kinsey, Wardell B. Pomeroy, and Clyde E. Martin, *Sexual Behavior in the Human Male* (Philadelphia, PA: W.B. Saunders, 1948), 57.

23. *Paris Adult Theatre v. Slaton*, 413 U.S. 39, 63 (1973).

24. Scott Yenor, "The Deregulation of pornography."

25. Matthew Larotonda, "Newsweek's Next Cover: Obama 'First Gay President'" *ABC News*, May 13, 2012, https://abcnews.go.com/blogs/politics/2012/05/newsweeks-next-cover-obama-first-gay-president.

26. Kevin Slack, "Liberalism Radicalized," *Heritage Foundation*, Aug. 27, 2013, https://www.heritage.org/political-process/report/liberalism-radicalized-the-sexual-revolution-multiculturalism-and-the-rise.

27. Scott Yenor, "The Deregulation of pornography."

28. Andrea Morris, "'God's Will Is No Concern of This Congress': NY Dem Jerry Nadler Rejects God During Equality Act Debate," *CBN*, Mar. 3, 2021, https://www2.cbn.com/news/us/gods-will-no-concern-congress-ny-dem-jerry-nadler-rejects-god-during-equality-act-debate.

CHAPTER 5: HONOR THE GOLDEN RULE, PART 1

1. Anthony Iaccarino, "The Founding Fathers and Slavery," *Encyclopedia Britannica*, September 7, 2023, https://www.britannica.com/topic/The-Founding-Fathers-and-Slavery-1269536.

2. "Three-fifths compromise," *Encyclopedia Britannica*, August 23, 2023, https://www.britannica.com/topic/three-fifths-compromise.

3. U.S. Const. art. I, § 2, cl. 3.

4. Angela Sailor, et al., "Slavery and the Constitution," *Heritage Foundation*, February 23, 2021, https://www.heritage.org/the-constitution/report/slavery-and-the-constitution.

5. U.S. Const. art. IV, § 2, cl. 3 ("No Person held to Service or Labour in one State, under the Laws thereof, escaping into another, shall, in Consequence of any Law or Regulation therein, be discharged from such Service or Labour, but shall be delivered up on Claim of the Party to whom such Service or Labour may be due.").

6. U.S. Const. art. I, § 8, cl. 1 ("The Migration or Importation of such Persons as any of the States now existing shall think proper to admit, shall not be prohibited by the Congress prior to the Year one thousand eight hundred and eight, but a Tax or duty may be imposed on such Importation, not exceeding ten dollars for each Person.").

7. "Today in History: July 9," *Library of Congress*, https://www.loc.gov/item/today-in-history/july-09/#a-constitution-for-vermont.

8. John Eidsmoe, *Christianity and the Constitution: The Faith of the Founding Fathers* (Grand Rapids, MI: Baker, 1987), 359.

9. Ibid.

10. Angela Sailor, "Slavery and the Constitution."

11. Ibid.

12. Ibid.

13. "Dred Scott Decision Causes and Effects," *Encyclopedia Britannica*, September 21, 2020, https://www.britannica.com/summary/Dred-Scott-Decision-Causes-and-Effects.

14. Ibid.

15. *Pierce v. Society of Sisters*, 268 U.S. 510 (1925).

16. In re *Winship*, 397 U.S. 358 (1970).

17. Angela Sailor, "Slavery and the Constitution," citing Damon Root, *A Glorious Liberty: Frederick Douglass and the Fight for an Anti-Slavery Constitution* (Lincoln, NE: University of Nebraska Press, 2020) 51-54, 64.

18. U.S. Const. amend. V; U.S. Const., art. I, §§ 9 & 10.

19. Angela Sailor, "Slavery and the Constitution."

20. U.S. Const. amend. IV.

21. U.S. Const. art. IV, § 2.

22. Angela Sailor, "Slavery and the Constitution."

23. *United States v. Fisher*, 6 U.S. (2 Cranch) 358, 390 (1805) ("Where rights are infringed, where fundamental principles are overthrown, where the general system of the laws is departed from, the legislative intention must be expressed with irresistible clearness to induce a court of justice to suppose a design to effect such objects."). See, e.g., *Atascadero State Hospital v. Scanlon*, 473 U.S. 234, 238–39 (1985); *Hilton v. S.C. Pub. Railways Comm'n*, 502 U.S. 197, 206 (1991); *Nevada Dep't of Human Res. v. Hibbs*, 538 U.S. 721, 726 (2003).

24. Angela Sailor, "Slavery and the Constitution."

25. "A Century of Lawmaking for a New Nation: U.S. Congressional Documents and Debates, 1774–1875," *Library of Congress*, https://memory.loc.gov/cgi-bin/ampage?collId=llsl&fileName=013/llsl013.db&recNum=804.

26. National Geographic Society, "The Black Codes and Jim Crow Laws," *National Geographic*, https://education.nationalgeographic.org/resource/black-codes-and-jim-crow-laws.

27. "Jim Crow Laws Causes and Effects," *Encyclopedia Britannica*, September 30, 2020, https://www.britannica.com/summary/Jim-Crow-Laws-Causes-and-Effects.

28. *Plessy v. Ferguson*, 163 U.S. 537, 552 (1896), overruled by *Brown v. Bd. of Ed. of Topeka*, 347 U.S. 483 (1954).

29. "Jim Crow Laws Causes and Effects," *Encyclopedia Britannica*.

30. "Jim Crow Laws," *History*, January 22, 2024, https://www.history.com/topics/early-20th-century-us/jim-crow-laws.

31. *Brown v. Bd. of Ed. of Topeka*, 347 U.S. 483, 493 (1954).

32. "Civil Rights Act," *Encyclopedia Britannica*, April 3, 2024, https://www.britannica.com/event/Civil-Rights-Act-United-States-1964.

33. "The Civil Rights Act of 1964: A Long Struggle for Freedom," *Library of Congress*, https://www
.loc.gov/exhibits/civil-rights-act/multimedia/hubert-humphrey-and-strom-thurmond.html.

34. Ibid.

35. Ibid.

36. *Heart of Atlanta Motel v. United States*, 379 U.S. 241 (1964).

37. *Masterpiece Cakeshop, Ltd. v. Colorado C.R. Commission*, 584 U.S. 617, 635 (2018).

38. *Bobby Jones University v. United States*, 461 U.S. 574 (1983).

39. *Bostock v. Clayton County*, 140 S. Ct. 1731 (2020).

CHAPTER 6: HONOR THE GOLDEN RULE, PART 2

1. Adam Cohen, *Imbeciles: The Supreme Court, American Eugenics, and the Sterilization of Carrie Buck* (New York: Penguin, 2017), 46.

2. "The Racist Roots of Planned Parenthood," *Johnson County Right to Life*, https://www.jcrtl
.org/planned-parenthoods-margaret-sanger.html.

3. Margaret Sanger, *The Pivot of Civilization in Historical Perspective: The Birth Control Classic* (Inkling Books, 2001), 274.

4. Margaret Sanger, *Birth Control Review*, April 1933.

5. "The Racist Roots of Planned Parenthood," *Johnson County Right to Life*.

6. L. Stoddard, *The Rising Tide of Color Against White World-Supremacy* (New York: Scribner's, 1920).

7. "The Racist Roots of Planned Parenthood," *Johnson County Right to Life*.

8. Cohen, *Imbeciles*, 2-4, 55-57.

9. Andrea DenHoed, "The Forgotten Lessons of the American Eugenics Movement," *The New Yorker*, April 27, 2016, https://www.newyorker.com/books/page-turner/the-forgotten-lessons-of-the
-american-eugenics-movement.

10. Cohen, *Imbeciles*, 4.

11. Ibid., see id., at 49-52; *Box v. Planned Parenthood of Indiana & Kentucky, Inc.*, 139 S. Ct. 1780, 1790 (2019).

12. *Buck v. Bell*, 274 U.S. 200 (1927).

13. Ibid., at 207.

14. *Box v. Planned Parenthood of Indiana & Kentucky, Inc.*, 139 S. Ct. 1780, 1786 (2019).

15. Cohen, *Imbeciles*, 299-300.

16. Cohen, *Imbeciles*, 319.

17. "The Racist Roots of Planned Parenthood," *Johnson County Right to Life*.

18. *Box v. Planned Parenthood of Indiana & Kentucky, Inc.*, 139 S. Ct. 1780, 1790 (2019).

19. *Box*, 1783.

20. *Roe v. Wade*, 410 U.S. 113, 153 (1973).

21. *Roe*, 410 U.S. at 158.

22. *Roe*, 410 U.S. at 159.

23. *Roe*, 410 U.S. at 154.

24. *Roe*, 410 U.S. at 154.

25. *Planned Parenthood v. Casey*, 505 U.S. 833 (1992).

26. John Conley, "Margaret Sanger was a eugenicist. Why are we still celebrating her?," *American Magazine*, November 27, 2017, https://www.americamagazine.org/politics-society/2017/11/27/margaret-sanger-was-eugenicist-why-are-we-still-celebrating-her.

27. Ibid.

28. Kay Cole James, "Even with Removing Margaret Sanger's Name, Planned Parenthood Is Still Influenced by Racist Founder," *Heritage Foundation*, July 29, 2020, https://www.heritage.org/life/commentary/even-removing-margaret-sangers-name-planned-parenthood-still-influenced-racist.

29. Margaret Sanger, *Woman and the New Race* (New York: Blue Ribbon, 1920), 229.

30. Kay Cole James, "Even with Removing Margaret Sanger's Name."

31. Camdyn Bruce, "Abrams fetal heartbeat comments draw GOP ire in House hearing," *The Hill*, September 29, 2022, https://thehill.com/policy/healthcare/3667896-abrams-fetal-heartbeat-comments-draw-gop-ire-in-house-hearing/.

32. *Box*, 139 S. Ct. at 1783.

33. *Box*, 139 S. Ct. at 1784.

34. O. Carter Snead, "The Supreme Court Should Protect Unborn Children with Down Syndrome," *Public Discourse*, January 2, 2019, https://www.thepublicdiscourse.com/2019/01/48245/; Melanie Israel, "The Supreme Court Delivered a Mixed Verdict on 2 Indiana Abortion Laws. Here's What That Means," *Heritage Foundation*, May 30, 2019, https://www.heritage.org/life/commentary/the-supreme-court-delivered-mixed-verdict-2-indiana-abortion-laws-heres-what-means.

35. Tyler Olson, "Senate Republicans force Dems to vote on CRT, fracking, abortion and more in marathon 'vote-a-rama,'" *Fox News*, August 11, 2021, https://www.foxnews.com/politics/senate-republicans-democrats-vote-a-rama-amendments-reconciliation.

36. O. Carter Snead, "The Supreme Court Should Protect Unborn Children with Down Syndrome."

37. Alexandra Desanctis, "What Did Ralph Northam Really Say about Abortion?," *National Review*, April 29, 2019, https://www.nationalreview.com/corner/what-did-ralph-northam-really-say-about-abortion/.

38. *Dobbs v. Jackson Women's Health Organization*, 597 U.S. 215 (2022).

39. *Roe*, 410 U.S. at 158.

40. C'Zar Bernstein, "The Constitutional Personality of the Unborn," *Journal Law, Economics, and Policy*, October 2023, 299.

41. Ibid.

42. Ibid.

43. *Dobbs v. Jackson Women's Health Organization*, 597 U.S. 215, xx (2022).

CHAPTER 7: LIVE WITH PURPOSE

1. Tony Evans, *Kingdom Agenda* (Chicago, IL: Moody, 1999), 29.

2. Ibid., 30.

3. Ibid., 28.

4. Ibid., 30, 31.

5. Ibid., 32.

6. Ibid., 29.

7. Ibid., 53.

8. John Locke, "An Essay Concerning Human Understanding" (Oxford: Clarendon Press, 1894), 348; "The Pursuit of Happiness," https://www.pursuit-of-happiness.org/history-of-happiness/john-locke/.

9. Ibid., 348.

10. Ibid., 258.

11. John Locke, "The Pursuit of Happiness."

12. Ibid.

13. Ibid.

14. Ibid.

15. Ibid.

16. John F. Kennedy, inaugural address, Washington, DC, January 20, 1961.

17. Brian J. Grim, "$1.2 Trillion Religious Economy in the U.S.," *Religious Freedom & Business Foundation*, https://religiousfreedomandbusiness.org/1-2-trillion-religious-economy-in-us, citing "The Socio-Economic Contributions of Religion to American Society: An Empirical Analysis," *Interdisciplinary Journal of Research on Religion*.

18. "Purpose in life and 8-year mortality by gender and race/ethnicity among older adults in the U.S.," *Preventative Medicine*, November 2022, https://www.sciencedirect.com/science/article/abs/pii/S0091743522003590#bb0130.

19. Ibid.

20. Grim, "$1.2 Trillion Religious Economy in the U.S."

21. Simon Turner, "End the Religious Tax Exemption," *The Wall Street Journal*, November 26, 2023, https://www.wsj.com/articles/church-end-the-religious-tax-exemption-b8d03df7.

CHAPTER 8: ESTABLISH JUSTICE

1. Tony Evans, *Kingdom Politics*, 61.

2. Ibid. at chapter 4. Righteousness must be the standard, as God has defined it. But correlating with righteousness comes justice. While righteousness is the standard of right and wrong, justice is the impartial and equitable application of God's moral law in society. It's possible to have righteous laws without a just application of those laws.

3. Brian A. Garner, *Black's Law Dictionary* (St. Paul, MN: Thomson Reuters, 2014).

4. Psalm 51:4; 1 John 3:4-8.

5. Mark Hill, *Christianity and Criminal Law* (London: Routledge, 2020), 280-281.

6. Ibid., 6.

7. Ibid., 1.

8. Ibid., 46-47.

9. Ibid., 57-58.

10. Ibid., 65, 67.

11. Ibid., 71.

12. U.S. Const. amend. XIII, emphasis added.

13. *Ruffin v. Commonwealth*, 62 Va. 790, 796 (1871).

14. Jerry Mitchell, "Lawmakers refused to increase an infamous prison's funding. Then, chaos erupted," *Mississippi Center for Investigative Reporting*, January 8, 2020, https://www.mississippi cir.org/news/lawmakers-refused-to-increase-an-infamous-prisons-funding.

15. Jerry Mitchell, "Lawmakers refused to increase an infamous prison's funding."

16. "Captive Labor: Exploitation of Incarcerated Workers," *ACLU and GHRC Research Report*, 2022, https://www.aclu.org/sites/default/files/field_document/2022-06-15-captivelaborresearchreport .pdf. Summary: https://www.aclu.org/news/human-rights/captive-labor-exploitation-of -incarcerated-workers.

17. Ibid.

18. Ibid.

19. Ibid.

20. Michelle Alexander, *The New Jim Crow* (New York: The New Press, 2010).

21. *13th*, directed by Ava Duvernay, Netflix, 2016, documentary.

22. Ibid.

23. Ibid.

24. Alexander, *The New Jim Crow*, 14.

25. *13th*.

26. "Forcing Black Men Out of Society," *The New York Times*, April 25, 2015, https://www.nytimes .com/2015/04/26/opinion/sunday/forcing-black-men-out-of-society.html.

27. *13th*.

28. *13th*.

29. *13th.*

30. Justin Wolfers, "1.5 Million Missing Black Men," *The New York Times*, April 20, 2015, https:// www.nytimes.com/interactive/2015/04/20/upshot/missing-black-men.html.

31. *13th.*

32. Curtis R. Blakely and Vic W. Bumphus, "Private and Public Sector Prisons—a Comparison of Select Characteristics," *Federal Probation: Journal of Correctional Philosophy and Practice*, https://www.uscourts.gov/sites/default/files/68_1_5_0.pdf.

33. Blackey, "Private and Public Sector Prisons."

34. Mackenzie Buday and Ashley Nellis, "Private Prisons in the United States," August 23, 2022, https://www.jstor.org/stable/resrep44120.

35. Udi Ofer, "How the 1994 Crime Bill Fed the Mass Incarceration Crisis," *ACLU*, https://www .aclu.org/news/smart-justice/how-1994-crime-bill-fed-mass-incarceration-crisis.

36. Ed Chung, "The 1994 Crime Bill Continues to Undercut Justice Reform—Here's How to Stop It," *American Progress*, https://www.americanprogress.org/article/1994-crime-bill-continues -undercut-justice-reform-heres-stop/; Ronald A. Young, "Mississippi Taxpayers Fund Welfare Payments to Private Prisons," *Prison Legal News*, November 15, 2001, https://www.prisonlegal news.org/news/2001/nov/15/mississippi-taxpayers-fund-welfare-payments-to-private-prisons/.

37. Ibid.

38. Ibid.

39. Z.L. Hajnal, "Why Does No One Vote in Local Elections?," *The New York Times*, October 22, 2018, https://www.nytimes.com/2018/10/22/opinion/why-does-no-one-vote-in-local-elections .html.

40. James C. Ho, "Pressure Is a Privilege: Judges, Umpires, and Ignoring the Booing of the Crowd," *Heritage Foundation Joseph Story Distinguished Lecture*, December 6, 2023, https://www.heritage .org/courts/report/pressure-privilege-judges-umpires-and-ignoring-the-booing-the-crowd.

41. *Trump v. Anderson*, 601 U.S. 100 (2024).

42. Neil Baron, "More justices, more piece: the push to expand the Supreme Court," *The Hill*, March 22, 2024, https://thehill.com/opinion/judiciary/4549746-more-justices-more-peace -the-push-to-expand-the-supreme-court/.

43. Ryan Doerfler and Samuel Moyn, "The Constitution Is Broken and Should Not Be Reclaimed," *The New York Times*, August 19, 2022, https://www.nytimes.com/2022/08/19/opinion/liberals -constitution.html.

44. Ketanji Brown Jackson, "Courage / Purpose / Authenticity: Black Women Leaders in the Civil Rights Movement Era and Beyond," University of Michigan Law School, Martin Luther King Jr. Day Celebration, University of Michigan Law School, Ann Arbor, Michigan (January 20, 2020), available at *U.S.S. Comm. on the Judiciary Questionnaire for Judicial Nominees, Attachments to Question 12(d), Ketanji Brown Jackson, Nominee to Be Associate Justice of the Supreme Court of the United States*, Comm. on the Judiciary, U.S. S., 117th Cong., 611 of 2086 (2022), https://www. judiciary.senate.gov/imo/media/doc/Jackson%20SJQ%20Attachments%20Final.pdf.

45. Timothy Keller, "What Is Justice in the Bible?," *Gospel in Life*, https://quarterly.gospelinlife .com/justice-in-the-bible/.

46. Mark Hill, Norman Doe, RH Helmholz, and John Witte Jr., eds., *Christianity and Criminal Law* (London: Routledge, 2020), 169-170, 172.

CHAPTER 9: LIBERATE EDUCATION

1. Aesop's Fable, "The Wolf in Sheep's Clothing," *Library of Congress*, https://www.read.gov/aesop/022.html.

2. See, for example, Matthew 13:3-9 (The Parable of the Sower); Matthew 13:31-32 (The Parable of the Mustard Seed); Luke 13:6-9 (The Barren Fig Tree); Luke 10:25-37 (The Parable of the Good Samaritan); Matthew 13:31-32; Mark 4:31-32; Luke 13:19 (The Grain of Mustard Seed); Luke 7:40-50 (The Two Debtors); Matthew 22:2-9; Luke 14:16-23 (The Great Banquet); Luke 15:11-32 (The Prodigal Son); Luke 16:19-31 (The Rich Man and Lazarus); Matthew 20:1-16 (Laborers in the Vineyard); Matthew 25:14-30; Luke 19:11-27 (The Talents); Matthew 24:32; Mark 13:28; Luke 21:29-30 (The Fig Tree).

3. Galatians 5:1—the apostle Paul, a convert who went from murdering Christians to Jesus' most persuasive advocate, said that it is for freedom that Christ has set us free; Acts 13:39—through Him everyone who believes is set free from every sin, a justification we were not able to obtain under the law of Moses; John 8:36—Jesus said that if the Son sets us free, we are free indeed (see the book of Romans especially 8:20-21).

4. Dr. Zachary Stein, "Education as Liberation: Education as Oppression: Education as First Philosophy," an excerpt from a paper currently in process: "On realizing the possibilities of emancipatory metatheory: beyond the cognitive maturity fallacy, toward an education revolution," http://www.zakstein.org/education-as-liberation-education-as-oppression-education-as-first-philosophy/.

5. Ibid.

6. See for example: John Taylor Gatto, *The Underground History of American Education*, https://www.youtube.com/watch?v=8_5h0aO8ZaE.

7. Caroline Downey, "American Students Lag behind Comparable Developing Countries in Math after Pandemic," *National Review*, December 6, 2023, https://www.nationalreview.com/news/american-students-lag-behind-comparable-developed-countries-in-math-after-pandemic/.

8. Hanna Skandera, "America's education system is failing—but a growing school choice movement believes it has the solution," *Forbes*, June 23, 2023, https://fortune.com/2023/06/23/americas-education-system-is-failing-but-a-growing-school-choice-movement-believes-it-has-the-solution/.

9. Fredrick Hess, "America's Students Flunk Civics and U.S. History on Nation's Report Card," *Forbes*, May 3, 2023, https://www.forbes.com/sites/frederickhess/2023/05/03/americas-students-flunk-civics-and-us-history-on-nations-report-card/?sh=2bbb21c15523.

10. Alessandra Malito, "Reading gap between wealthy and poor students widens, study says," *NBC News*, January 28, 2014, http://usnews.nbcnews.com/_news/2014/01/28/22471408-reading-gap-between-wealthy-and-poor-students-widens-study-says?lite.

11. Carla Amurao, "Fact Sheet: How Bad Is the School-to-Prison Pipeline?," *Tavis Smiley Reports*, http://www.pbs.org/wnet/tavissmiley/tsr/education-under-arrest/school-to-prison-pipeline-fact-sheet/.

12. "Schoolkids in Handcuffs," *The New York Times*, November 4, 2015, http://www.nytimes.com/2015/11/04/opinion/schoolkids-in-handcuffs.html?_r=0.

13. Carla Amurao, "Fact Sheet: How Bad Is the School-to-Prison Pipeline?"

14. "Dismantling the School to Prison Pipeline," *NAACP Legal Defense Fund*, http://www.naacpldf .org/files/case_issue/Dismantling_the_School_to_Prison_Pipeline.pdf; Laura Moser, "Georgia Sends Kids with Disabilities and Behavior Problems to Special Schools. That's Segregation," *Slate*, July 31, 2015, https://slate.com/human-interest/2015/07/georgia-schools-investigation -too-many-kids-are-getting-sent-to-special-schools.html.

15. "Literary Statistics," *Begin to Read*, http://www.begintoread.com/research/literacystatistics.html.

16. Charles Kenny, "The Real Reason America's Schools Stink," *Bloomberg*, August 19, 2012, http:// www.bloomberg.com/bw/articles/2012-08-19/the-real-reason-americas-schools-stink.

17. Betsy DeVos, *Hostages No More: The Fight for Education Freedom and the Future of the American Child* (New York: Hachette, 2022), 205.

18. Ibid., 206, footnote 13.

19. Ibid., footnote 21.

20. Allie Bidwell, "Most US Students Live in or Near Poverty," *US News and World Report*, January 16, 2015, http://www.usnews.com/news/blogs/data-mine/2015/01/16/most-us-students -come-from-low-income-families.

21. Lindsey Cook, "U.S. Education: Still Separate and Unequal," *US News and World Report*, January 28, 2015, http://www.usnews.com/news/blogs/data-mine/2015/01/28/us-education -stillseparate-and-unequal.

22. DeVos, *Hostages No More,* 206.

23. Ibid.

24. Ibid., 210.

25. P. Hemez, J.J. Brent, T.J. Mowen, "Exploring the School-to-Prison Pipeline: How School Suspensions Influence Incarceration During Young Adulthood," *Youth Violence Juv Justice*, July 18, 2020, 235-255.

26. Alexander, *The New Jim Crow*, 21.

27. Ibid.

28. Ibid.

29. Danny McLoughlin, "US Prison Literacy Statistics," *WordsRated*, June 2, 2023, https://words rated.com/us-prison-literacy-statistics/.

30. Amurao, "Fact Sheet: How Bad Is the School-to-Prison Pipeline?"

31. Stein, "Education as Liberation: Education as Oppression: Education as First Philosophy."

32. Ibid.

33. Frederick Douglass wrote this in 1855 in reference to a series of dialogues he had with white slave owners who simply did not see, in any way, that slavery was a moral and absolute wrong.

34. Lindsey M. Burke, Jonathan Butcher, Jay P. Greene, eds., "The Critical Classroom: How Critical Race Theory Undermines Academic Excellence and Individual Agency in Education," *Heritage Foundation*, 2022, https://capefearbeacon.com/wp-content/uploads/2023/08/2022 -The-Critical-Classroom_FINAL_WEB-Heritage-Foundation.pdf.

35. Michelle Alexander, Facebook, September 19, 2016.

36. "Michelle Alexander, 'The New Jim Crow' Author, Explains Her Transition From Law to Religion," *Faithfully Magazine*, September 19, 2016, https://faithfullymagazine.com/michelle-alexander-new-jim-crow-author-explains-transition-law-religion/.

37. Alfred Kinsey, *Sexual Behavior in the Human Male* (Bloomington, IN: Indiana University Press 1984).

38. *The Mind Polluters* documentary, directed by Mark Archer, 2021.

39. Robert Knight, "Fraud and Pervert Alfred C. Kinsey Returns," *Washington Times*, September 24, 2022, https://www.washingtontimes.com/news/2022/sep/24/fraud-and-pervert-alfred-c-kinsey-returns/.

40. Ibid.

41. Ibid.

42. Ibid.

43. *The Mind Polluters*.

44. Ronna McDaniel, "Democrats Want to Raise Your Kids. Republicans Fight for Parental Rights," *Newsweek*, May 10, 2022, https://www.newsweek.com/democrats-want-raise-your-kids-republicans-fight-parental-rights-opinion-1704862.

45. Conor Friedersdorf, "Is Defying Parents the Only Ethical Alternative?," *The Atlantic*, January 10, 2023.

46. Mary Harrington, "Normophobia," *Newsessential Blog*, April 3, 2024, https://newsessentials.wordpress.com/2024/04/03/normophobia/.

47. Mary Harrington, "Normophobia," *First Things*, April 2024, https://www.firstthings.com/article/2024/04/normophobia.

48. Pete Hegseth and David Goodwin, *Battle for the American Mind: Uprooting a Century of Miseducation* (New York: Broadside Books, 2022), 78-79.

49. DeVos, *Hostages No More*, 211.

50. Ibid., 199.

51. Ibid., 127.

52. Ibid.

53. Ibid., 128.

54. Ibid.

55. Jason L. Riley, "Charter Schools' Success Makes Them a Political Target," *The Wall Street Journal*, December 13, 2022, https://www.wsj.com/articles/charter-schools-success-makes-them-a-political-target-supreme-court-dress-code-lawsuit-education-aclu-teachers-unions-11670968061.

56. Ibid.

57. Ibid.

58. DeVos, *Hostages No More*, 200.

59. Ibid.

60. Ibid., 198.

61. Ibid., 225.

62. Hegseth and Goodwin, *Battle for the American Mind*, 49.

CHAPTER 10: SPEAK AND RECOGNIZE TRUTH

1. George Orwell, *Nineteen Eighty-Four* (New York: Signet Classic, 1950), 1.

2. Rod Dreher, *Live Not by Lies* (New York: Sentinel, 2020), 25.

3. Ibid.

4. Ibid., 28.

5. *Third Reich: The Rise*, directed by Seth Skundrick, History Channel, 2010, TV mini-series.

6. Ibid.

7. Ibid.

8. Ibid., 24:39.

9. Ibid.

10. Ibid.

11. Ibid.

12. Ibid.

13. Ibid.

14. Beina Xu and Eleanor Albert, "Media Censorship in China," *Council on Foreign Relations*, February 17, 2017, https://www.cfr.org/backgrounder/media-censorship-china.

15. Ibid.

16. "Google turns off China Censorship Warning," *BBC News*, January 7, 2013, https://www.bbc.com/news/technology-20932072.

17. Xu, "Media Censorship in China."

18. Ibid.

19. Collin Perkel, "Media 'under threat': Canada slips out of Top 20 in press freedom index," *Canada's National Observer*, April 26, 2017, https://www.nationalobserver.com/2017/04/26/news/media-under-threat-canada-slips-out-top-20-press-freedom-index.

20. "Canadian reporter faces charges after covering protests," *Committee to Protect Journalists*, March 17, 2017, https://cpj.org/2017/03/canadian-reporter-faces-charges-after-covering-pro/.

21. Rachael Thomas, "Free Speech is under attack in Canada," *Lethbridge Herald*, May 7, 2022, https://lethbridgeherald.com/commentary/opinions/2022/05/07/free-speech-is-under-attack-in-canada/.

22. The Future of Media Project, "Canadian Media Ownership Index," *Harvard University*, February 12, 2022, https://projects.iq.harvard.edu/futureofmedia/canadian-media-ownership.

23. Abraham Blondeau, "The CBC and Canada's State-sponsored Media," *The Trumpet*, January 11, 2022, https://www.thetrumpet.com/25075-the-cbc-and-canadas-state-sponsored-media.

24. Ibid.

25. Ibid.

26. "Freedom of expression and media freedom," *Government of Canada*, https://www.international.gc.ca/world-monde/issues_development-enjeux_developpement/human_rights-droits_homme/freedom_expression_media-liberte_expression_medias.aspx?lang=eng.

27. Blondeau, "The CBC and Canada's State-sponsored Media"; Kait Bolongaro, "Trudeau's Party Passes Bill to Regulate Social Media, Streaming," *Bloomberg*, June 22, 2021, https://www.bloomberg.com/news/articles/2021-06-22/trudeau-s-party-passes-bill-to-regulate-social-media-streaming?leadSource=uverify%20wall#xj4y7vzkg.

28. "The Role of Christian Media: Deciphering the media landscape and finding our calling within," *Christianweek*, January 30, 2022, https://www.christianweek.org/the-role-of-christian-media/.

29. Wesley J. Smith, "Canada Stifles Religious Freedom," *National Review*, June 28, 2019, https://www.nationalreview.com/corner/canada-stifles-religious-freedom/.

30. Bob Kuhn, "Canada Attacks Religious Freedom," *The Wall Street Journal*, June, 21, 2018, https://www.wsj.com/articles/canada-attacks-religious-freedom-1529623475; Wesley Smith, "Canada Stifles Religious Freedom," *National Review*, June 28, 2019.

31. Jorge Gomez, "Canada's Crackdown on Religious Freedom Is a Wake-Up Call for Americans," *First Liberty*, March 11, 2022, https://firstliberty.org/news/canada-crackdown-wake-up-call-for-americans/.

32. Ibid.

33. Robert Hassan, "Guide to the classics: Orwell's *1984* and how it helps us understand tyrannical power today," *The Conversation*, April 29, 2019, https://theconversation.com/guide-to-the-classics-orwells-1984-and-how-it-helps-us-understand-tyrannical-power-today-112066.

34. Kristine Parks, "Sen. Hawley debating Berkeley law professor over pregnant men blows up Twitter," *Fox News*, July 12, 2022, https://www.foxnews.com/media/sen-hawley-debating-berkeley-law-professor-pregnant-men-blows-up-twitter.

35. "Memorandum," *Public Opinion Strategies*, https://pos.org/wp-content/uploads/2022/03/POS-National-Poll-Release-Memo.pdf; Keisha Toni Russell, "Picking a fight with moms and dads," *World*, November 7, 2022, https://wng.org/opinions/picking-a-fight-with-moms-and-dads-1667821659.

36. "America has a free speech problem," *The New York Times*, March 18, 2022, https://www.nytimes.com/2022/03/18/opinion/cancel-culture-free-speech-poll.html.

37. Emily Ekins, "The State of Free Speech and Tolerance in America Attitudes About Free Speech, Campus Speech, Religious Liberty, and Tolerance of Political Expression," *Cato Institute*, October 31, 2017, https://www.cato.org/survey-reports/state-free-speech-tolerance-america#overview.

38. Rod Dreher, *Live Not by Lies*, 35.

39. Colleen McClain, "More so than adults, U.S. teens value people feeling safe online over being able to speak freely," *Pew Research*, August 30, 2022, https://www.pewresearch.org/fact-tank/2022/08/30/more-so-than-adults-u-s-teens-value-people-feeling-safe-online-over-being-able-to-speak-freely/.

40. Dreher, *Live Not by Lies*, 3.

41. Orwell, *Nineteen Eighty-Four*, 205.

42. Miles Parks, "Social Media Usage Is At An All-Time High. That Could Mean A Nightmare For Democracy," *NPR*, May 22, 2020, https://www.npr.org/2020/05/27/860369744/social-media-usage-is-at-an-all-time-high-that-could-mean-a-nightmare-for-democr.

43. Kuhn, "Canada Attacks Religious Freedom."

44. Aaron Earls, "Christian or Mainstream Media: Which Do Evangelicals Prefer?," *Lifeway Research*, April 1, 2022, https://research.lifeway.com/2022/04/01/christian-or-mainstream-media-which-do-evangelicals-prefer/.

CHAPTER 11: TAKE THE STAND

1. Lee Strobel, *The Case for Christ* (Grand Rapids, MI: Zondervan, 2016), 61.

2. Ibid., 63.

3. Ibid.

4. Ibid.

5. Ibid., 171, 178.

ABOUT THE AUTHOR

Keisha Toni Russell is a constitutional lawyer with First Liberty Institute in Texas, a nonprofit law firm that specializes in religious liberty litigation. She has also worked as a federal law clerk on the Fifth Circuit Court of Appeals, which covers judicial districts in Mississippi, Louisiana, and Texas.

Keisha is a sought-after speaker who has written op-eds in various national news outlets and delivered commentary on TV networks like CBS, Fox News, CBN, the Victory Channel, and others.

Keisha graduated from Emory University School of Law and was a 2017 Emory University Graduating Woman of Excellence. Prior to becoming a lawyer, Keisha was a special education teacher in an elementary school in Atlanta, Georgia.

Keisha grew up in Palm Beach County, Florida, and currently resides in Dallas, Texas.

SCRIPTURE VERSIONS USED IN THIS BOOK

To learn more about Harvest House books and
to read sample chapters, visit our website:

www.HarvestHousePublishers.com

HARVEST HOUSE PUBLISHERS
EUGENE, OREGON